From Baghdad to Berkeley
A Woman's Affair

Nadia Al-Samarrie

Disclaimer
Some names and identifying details have been
changed to protect the privacy of individuals.

Cover Design by Nadia Al-Samarrie

Editor- Nathaniel Mellor

Editor- Mary Ruth Yao

Dedication

Coming to America, I was blessed with family, teachers, coaches, friends, and a former husband who believed in me in ways that I had yet to discover. Their kindness and compassion guided me through turbulent times. I had no idea what it was like to be American, let alone a Berkeley girl.

My American and foreign family and friends have enriched my life with their unconditional love and support, fueling me to forge ahead during difficult and turbulent times. They cheered me on when I couldn't find the light in the dark tunnel.

My elementary school teacher, Mrs. West, motivated me to learn beyond my framework. Her inspiration became a lifelong building block that I am still playing with. My swim team coach, Aggi from Willard Junior High, taught me that coming in last place was just the beginning. My English teacher, Johnny Selvin from Berkeley High, opened the door to a writing style that allowed me to emote in ways I did not know were possible. Mrs. Wilson, also from Berkeley High, put my classroom curriculum aside to validate my undercover investigation efforts regardless of my frequent voluntary absence from her class. I had no idea how Mr. and Mrs. Sussman, with their daughter Margit's one-year sabbatical in Berkeley, would forever alter the course of my life with positive experiences.

My grandmother, Bibi, whom I still miss, taught me to laugh at myself. My father freed me from the cultural obligations of being a Middle Eastern woman. My mother modeled strength and adventure during adversity. Together they defied their cultural norms, setting the stage for racism to have no place in our bicultural home. My siblings, John, Mimi, and Jamal—I cannot imagine my life without them. We were a tribe of four, traveling foreign lands like Vikings, uncertain of what challenges the next territory would bring.

My former husband, Scott, a business partner, the father of my children, pushed me to be my better self. He encouraged me to walk through my fears, giving me the strength to keep growing personally and professionally.

My children, Spencer and Miranda, whom I love more than they could ever imagine, have enriched my life in being so darn American.

Table of Contents

Introduction

Some people consider my hometown Berkeley, California, as a subculture of America. I lack the objectivity that other Americans have about a city that carries a politically volatile history, archived in books as a place where social change transformed politics, fashion, and culture.

Berkeley was a place where I could be myself unencumbered by my family name, culture, or religious expectation. I was a "nobody" and loved being invisible when my actions went unnoticed. I was no longer concerned with the implications of how I stood, if my laughter was too loud, what I was wearing, how I was behaving, and what it meant to my father's family or his dignitary colleagues.

I came from a life where what people thought of you was more dangerous than what you did. My life in Berkeley gifted me with a rebirth where my culture, wealth, and heritage carried no weight as a young girl growing up in America. It merely made me novel as an American who was raised abroad with a foreign father. That kind of background made no difference in Berkeley.

My unbiased life in America includes a Chinese uncle whom my aunt married in the 1950s, a Native American aunt I've never met, and an African American aunt from the 1960s I loved. In 1953, my mother married my father, an Arab. My brother continued the family tradition of diversity by marrying a Jewish woman in the 1980s.

Growing up in a culturally diverse environment introduced me to different languages, cultures, lifestyles, and spiritual practices that influenced me. My innocence shielded me from society's prejudices because my culturally diverse family was like any other family. We enjoyed holidays, meals, good times, and bad times.

Growing up, defining normal, seemed to be an evolving continuum. As a result of my life experiences, I have a great threshold for tolerance, diversity in culture, and spirituality. The life that I choose to live today is a result of the lifestyles and cultures I have been privy to.

In 2017 I was at the Findhorn Foundation in Scotland attending a program when a facilitator asked my group, "How do you refer to yourself? A woman? Mother? Father?" I raised my hand to ask, "What if I don't see myself with any of these labels?" A fellow student asked me, "Where is your vulnerability to this question?"

I responded, "I see myself as a spirit, not as my profession, not as a woman, not as a divorcee, or a mother." I am a person with a spirit that is defined by my unique global and cultural life experiences. These are the lenses that I see myself and other people through. It is something I have experienced my whole life.

Americans see me as an Arab. Arabs see me as an American. When I was a financial consultant, my colleagues viewed me as a woman. When I lived in Oakland, some saw me as a white woman. When I speak of my maternal McFeeley side, some see me as an Irish descendent. When I share that I was raised in Berkeley, some see me as a liberal. When I was at my graduation dinner for a financial consulting program, a man from Middle America could not hold back from telling me that I was from the "cesspool of liberalism."

All these labels have ushered in both welcome and unwelcome experiences. People's attitudes toward me often reflect their cultural values from a geographical location that confines them by definition. Being embraced or rejected by them is based on whether they viewed me as a threat or an expansion to their social and family values.

When I traveled the world as a Californian, people were either intrigued or repelled by me, depending on which state or country they grew up in. As a single female traveling the world alone at different ages and stages in my life, I have learned a lot about diverse cultural values, politics, men's views on women, and societal tolerance. The lessons were both liberating and sometimes life-threatening.

How we are framed can either limit or expand our horizon based on our sex, race, gender, and sexual preference. Traveling around the world at a young age allowed me to embrace or reject the limitations and the biased labels society brands us with.

class photo of me in first grade in Baghdad

my best friends - John, Mimi, Jamal and I

looking groovy in 1975

top left- Jean, mom, Mimi, myself, John below me and Jamal to his left

my Uncle Munam and Father with me at the Al-Samarrie Mosque in Baghdad

Mc Feeley family roots trip in Ireland with Mimi and John

Scotland at the Clava Cairns

Chapter 1
Moving to Tehran, Iran, in 1966

My father was stationed in Iran at the Iraqi Embassy in 1966. I was eight years old. For three years, we lived in Tehran, attending a Persian Iraqi school with a bicultural network of friends.

Later, our friendships expanded even further when we joined the American Club. Families from all over the world that were stationed in Iran were members of the club. They were mostly families with Christian wives and Muslim husbands. They celebrated all the Christian holidays at the club and Muslim holidays with their paternal family.

I remember when we first arrived in our new home in Iran. I walked down to the corner store from our three-story house that had a blue, mosaic koi pond with three fish. I wanted to buy pistachios even though I could not speak the language. Determined to go on my first solo expedition, I approached the big double iron gate, exiting the courtyard. I tried to fit in by walking down the street casually, wondering if I looked like a foreigner. At that time, I was an Iraqi expat who did not realize that my red-blondish hair, blue eyes, and light skin tone made me stand out.

Stepping out onto the street by myself, I felt a new sense of freedom. Something was very different, and I knew it. For the first time in my life, I was allowed to go to the store without a chaperone.

In Baghdad, our driver took us to our destination. The maids cleaned our home; the guards secured the exterior of our compound. We were surrounded by hired help with constraints, unable to leave our home unaccompanied— that is, unless we were with our mother.

While walking down the street, I was elated. My inability to speak Farsi did not prevent me from going to the store to buy a treat. I figured scooping pistachios into a brown bag by the kilo would not require much in language skills. One block from my new home, I stood outside the store, staring at the gunny sacks of nuts and beans that sat outside the store entrance. I reached for a brown bag, scooping pistachios into it. Walking to the cash register to pay, my right hand was rummaging in my pockets for a new, unfamiliar currency, the Rial. I handed my bag to the man behind the counter to weigh the pistachios. He leaned over the cash register, looked down at me, and told me what I owed in Farsi. I did not understand a word he said, handing him a bill, trying to look confident. He gave me my change with a look that questioned my fluency.

Walking out of the store, the sudden feeling of victory overpowered me. I felt accomplished. My inability to speak the local language did not prevent me from pursuing what I wanted.

This victorious feeling, in retrospect, was momentous, something that I started to build on throughout my life, by never allowing what I don't know to prevent me from pursuing what I want. I have since learned that my desires come with as much failure as success. It's the nature of life.

I loved living in Iran. We had one maid, no driver, no guards. Life felt lighter, with fewer people overseeing every move we made. This, of course, did not apply when my parents hosted dignitary events. Nor did it apply when we attended dignitary events with political leaders from the Middle East whose names grace political science books.

My father's job was to stimulate commerce between Iran and Iraq. He traveled excessively to different locations, visiting large scale plants to negotiate exporting and importing trade deals for Iraq. When the Prime Minister of Iraq, Abdul- Rahman Arif, visited Iran, my parents would go to the airport and stand on the tarmac, in a welcoming line to shake his hand. They would then join him at his public appearance.

Women dressed elegantly back in the 1960s. The Shah's third wife, Farrah, brought Italian fashion to Iran. Cultured women of means aspired to her fashion standards. Men and women dressed more like Westerners, a dramatic departure from today's tribal style.

Life in Iran was busy and fun. When the Iraqi soccer team played Iran, we sat in the front with the players. It was exciting to be on the front lines for a national sport that evoked a plethora of emotions.

We settled into our new school. My siblings spoke two languages, with their third language being Farsi. I was the youngest of the four and never learned to speak English until we came to the United States.

Living in Tehran offered independence that I had not experienced in Baghdad. I was able to have a bicycle, new-found freedom with wheels to visit people and places. This was the second milestone for me. When I was a young girl, my Iraqi family did not allow me to have a bicycle or go anywhere.

We went to the American club in Iran frequently to swim. After the sunset in the hot summers, an American general hosted an event for the children. He would throw dozens of coins into the pool for fun. All the children who were able to swim jumped in before the coins could hit the bottom of the pool. Swimming without goggles, we could still see and catch the coins as they were sinking to the pool's undersurface. The thrill of collecting the currency allowed us to buy Hershey's candy bars, drink Coca Cola, and buy American comic books without asking our parents for money.

Sometimes Jamal, the younger of my two brothers, and I used our coins from the pool game to play the slot machine when the staff and adults were distracted. Occasionally, we would hit what we perceived as the jackpot, with one of us guarding our activity. At the same time, the other struggled to collect the coins from the slot machine. When we won, the money would come out quicker than we could catch it.

Movie nights at the club exposed us to Doris Day, Rock Hudson, Jerry Lewis, Dean Martin, James Bond, and the frightening Phantom of the Opera movie. I remember sitting on my father's lap, unable to watch the Phantom's jaw-clenching scenes. The dark and scary opera building that the Phantom inhabited scared me. Every time he surfaced, I hid my face in my father's jacket, waiting for the scene to end. I could understand the movies, but I could not speak English. Back then, I was fluent in Arabic and later fluent in Farsi.

At home on TV, we watched Yogi Bear, Casper, The Flintstones, and Betty Boop. In the evenings, we watched Mission Impossible, Dark Shadows, Outer Limits, and The Monkees. I used to play The Monkees' music, imitating their energetic dancing style. No one in the Middle East danced like that.

It snowed in the winter in Iran. My mother decided that we would learn how to ski. She ordered skis from Germany for us. We took skiing lessons at Shemshak and Ab Ali, two big ski resorts near Tehran.

One year, my Aunt Grace, with her three children, joined us from Baghdad. My mother and Aunt Grace knew each other from their double dating days with their Iraqi husbands in 1950s Berkeley, before they moved to Baghdad. The winter that Aunt Grace came to Iran, our mothers hired a ski instructor for the seven of us at the resort. With no ski lifts to sit on, we were left with a moving rope with handles; getting up the mountain took effort for a beginner but getting to the top with your skis and poles was the first step in learning how to ski.

Shemshak that winter was my first recollection of being so cold that my fingers felt like they were going to fall off. I had to keep my gloves on the entire time. Our lessons did not last long. One day I watched the ski instructor quit because teaching three seven-year-olds, two eight-year-olds, one ten-year-old, and a thirteen-year-old brought many unprepared challenges. In a tense exchange, he threw the money he'd been paid to teach us back at my aunt. From a distance, the currency floated like feathers onto the snowy ground.

In 1969 tension started to build over Shatt al-Arab River, a waterway that Iraq and Iran have accessed with water rights that date back for centuries. This was the beginning of Iran's government's intolerance with Iraqi expats living in their country.

Since we were dignitaries living in Tehran, our car had Iraqi Embassy license plates. The changing political climate led to us being targeted by the local authorities. If we parked and left our car, it would be the only car that received a parking violation upon our return to the vehicle.

The political tension continued to build. Iraqis were being visited at their homes by the Persian authorities asking them to leave. My parents knew it was just a matter of time before receiving a knock on the door. In a proactive move, they sold everything. My father was transferred to London. My mother seized the opportunity to bring us back to the United States. Secretly, she wanted to divorce my father. Knowing that she would have no legal rights to her children in the Middle East, divorce meant walking away from her children, a price she was unwilling to pay.

My father was transferred to London. He maintained his position with the Embassy. Shortly after he settled in the United Kingdom, a new edict was passed down by the Iraqi government. Anyone married to a foreigner had to divorce their partner or give up their position in the Iraqi Embassy. My mother, on the other hand, was elated to be back on American soil finally. We landed at JFK in New York after vacationing in Lebanon. She hired a limo to accommodate the five of us with our luggage to her sister's home.

Coming to America was a different experience—another new country with a different language. But this time, we had family on my mother's side to join. My expectations of America were filtered through the movies I watched at the American Club in Iran. We arrived at our Aunt Mary Grace's home in June of 1969. Like my mother, Aunt Mary Grace married a foreign man in the 1950s. My Uncle Ken came from Northern China.

I had no sense of what it meant to be bicultural. It was the only life I knew. Everyone we associated with abroad had one parent who came from another country. Our shared social thread was our Muslim fathers. My Chinese Irish cousins were normal in my world. We shared Irish heritage, just like we shared an Iraqi culture with my cousins in Baghdad. I expected us to be different and the same.

Our Irish mothers, eight years apart, were the matriarchs of the family. They ruled their family through their Catholic values. Aunt Mary Grace was a devoted Catholic. My mother turned against her church at a young age after her Jewish best friend passed away, and her Catholic school forbade her from going to her friend's funeral. Even though my mother did not attend church, she went through Catholic schools up to her college years. Christianity influenced her beliefs of right and wrong and what was accepted as social behavior.

Aunt Mary, my Irish grandfather's sister, did not approve of my Uncle Ken's marriage to my aunt. She asked my aunt to think of what her children would go through as biracial kids. Knowing her Aunt Mary's response to her sister's marriage, my mother eloped with my father. She did not dare to tell her aunt that she married a Muslim Arab. When she visited Aunt Mary, my mother introduced my father, her husband, as a friend. Dad went along with it, maybe because his family had yet to be informed that he was married to an Irish Christian American.

We spent a month with my aunt, uncle, and eight cousins in Maryland. They had a large home that accommodated us all. I loved meeting my cousins and sharing meals, crafts, and sports with them. They are all interesting people. Even though we don't see much of each other as adults given our geographical distance, they continue to be important people in my life.

We started on our next venture, driving across the country to California in a blue station wagon with four rambunctious kids in the car. Anytime we didn't listen to our mother, she would take one shoe off while driving, look in the mirror, and, with perfect aim, throw her shoe at the disobeying child.

People stared at us when we stopped to eat at restaurants, not because we looked different, but because we spoke Arabic at the table. In the Middle East, we looked different but spoke like natives in Iraq and Iran. Now that I understand the cultural differences between the Midwest and California, we must have seemed like passing gypsies, entertaining the locals with our foreign tongue.

Mom could not wait to get to Stockton, a place where she spent a lot of time with her aunt and uncle, whom she adored. When my mother pulled off the street with her baby blue station wagon to park, my brother Jamal ran to the front door wanting to be the first. Mom organized us from youngest to eldest before we rang the doorbell. Jamal and I stood in the front, next to each other, pushing one another. We both rang the doorbell at the same time while pushing each other to be first. A tall man answered the door. Before we had a chance to introduce ourselves, he turned to a sign below the bell, pointed, and said, "Can't you read the sign? No solicitors."

My mom's voice from behind hollered, "Uncle Rex, it's me, Carol." My uncle looked up and gave us a big smile. He was excited to see us.

"Come in, come in," he said. Aunt Miriam ran into the living room from the kitchen to greet us; she made us all feel welcomed.

Aunt Miriam was an elementary school teacher. Uncle Rex had a bar and vending machine business. As children, we delighted in his candy inventory from his vending machines. We could have as much candy as we wanted or choose one toy without putting coins in the machine. Jamal and I were in heaven. Life in California gave us a new sense of security. My great aunt and uncle hosted us at their home as long as Mom needed us to be there.

My mother's brother, Uncle Charles, came by to take us out. Even though I did not know his profession, I felt he did something like my dad. He worked for the government. In which capacity, I did not know. It appeared to me that he was using us as a cover to scope out a building. He was showing up with young children who were not his. Dad was a dignitary; Uncle Charles seemed to have a covert profession.

Uncle Charles spent his life working for the U.S. government. He joined the military at a young age, passing away two years after he retired. During World War II, he was a prisoner in a camp near Frankfurt named Stalag 13. You may remember it from the TV show Hogan's Heroes. The day my uncle was to be executed was the day the war ended. He was held captive for five years. Uncle Charles was a fascinating man. I believe he was a spy for many years. Although none of this was shared with us, things like having a trunk with sophisticated radio gear told us he was not the average enlistee. As spies go, there was no confirmation for his title. But one family member who worked in a different military branch explained that the radio gear Uncle Charles had suggested what his profession entailed.

As a bicultural niece, what stood out to me most about my uncle was that he was the only sibling who married someone from his race, a

Caucasian woman. At the age of ten, I remember thinking that it was interesting.

My mother wanted to live in the Bay Area after leaving Aunt Miriam and Uncle Rex's home in Stockton. We drove around to many different places. In the end, she decided to raise us in Alameda, California, where her cousin Ann from Ireland had chosen to settle to raise her family.

We drove up to our new home, full of excitement and anticipation. The landlord stood there, waiting to greet us. We all walked to the front door. The landlord asked my mother where her husband was. She informed him that her husband was in London, that he would not be moving in with us until later. The landlord, a Caucasian man, blocked the front door to inform my mother that she could not move in without her husband. Even though I could not articulate it, the feeling of discrimination was familiar to me as a bicultural daughter.

In some ways, living in Iran prepared me for my new life in America. I grew up watching American movies and television shows that redefined a new "normal." I no longer lived in a white ivory tower compound, overshadowed by an Iraqi code of conduct. It was like going from a fishbowl to an open ocean.

Jamal and I celebrating our birthdays at the American Club with mom serving cake

Jamal and I in Tehran on the roof of our home

Jamal dad and I in Tehran

Jamal, John and I in Tehran

Brother John shaking hands with Iraqi President Abdul Rahman Arif -
Shaw of Iran on the far left

mom and dad greeting the President of Iraq Abdul- Rahman Arif and his
wife on the tarmac in Tehran

mom at a reception with Faika - wife of Abdul- Rahman Arif President of Iraq

ski resort in Iran with mom, Jamal, Mimi and friends

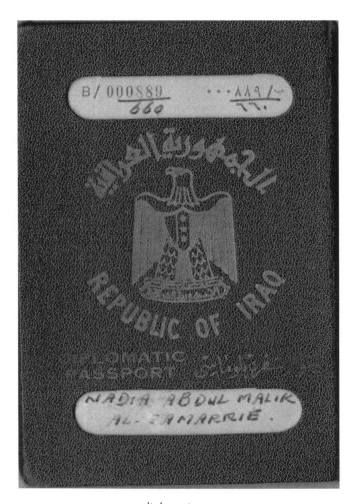

my diplomatic passport

top left to right- David, Uncle Ken, Ken, John, Joe, Aunt Mary Grace.
Margaret, Jamal, Mimi, Mom. Liz, Barbara, Carolyn/Dusty, Paul and me

photo by Ken Yale

FROM BAGHDAD TO BERKELEY

Chapter 2
Culturally Unaware of Racial Tensions

My poor mother. Imagine pulling up in a station wagon with a U-Haul and four children, excited about starting a new life only to be turned away at the last minute because the landlord would not rent to a woman without her husband being there.

My resilient, headstrong, Irish mother did not indulge in self-pity. She pulled out the newspaper and found a place we could move into within one day. It was a beautiful, white, Victorian house with a white picket fence and a large backyard. My sister and I shared one room; everyone else had their own room. Jamal planted the most beautiful vegetable garden in the back. He was very proud of his harvest at the tender age of eleven.

Mom enrolled three of us in a Catholic school. My brother John went to a private high school in San Francisco. It was a significant change from the Muslim schools we attended. My middle name changed from Abdul Malik to Ann. Jamal and I were both born in Baghdad, which is why we have Arab names. My siblings John and Mimi were born in the San Francisco Bay Area, hence their American names.

On the first day of school, I wore the traditional Catholic school uniform: plaid skirt, white shirt, white stockings, with a blue blazer. I was accustomed to wearing a uniform to school. In the Middle East, we wore a grey skirt, white shirts, and blue blazers. Similar to the Middle East, we also lined up outside on the playground until our teacher came to lead us into our class. Unlike my school days overseas, at Catholic school I always felt anxious. Unable to read, write, or speak English, communicating was impossible. Consequently, I was held back one grade.

On my first day of fourth grade, I was seated in the first row closest to the door. The teacher scribbled on the blackboard with white chalk from left to right. Lost in the exercise, I had no idea what I was supposed to do. I couldn't ask or follow along. I watched the other students as they lifted the top of their desks to take a piece of paper and a pencil out. They seemed to understand what is required of them. I had no idea what was expected of me. What made it more confusing for me is that Arabic is written from right to left. I could not pick up on the visual cues. The circles she made from left to right were never-ending. I couldn't even begin to duplicate her drawing. I was accustomed to different letters of the alphabet. In frustration, I raised my hand, gesturing my need to leave, hoping she knew that I meant I wanted to go to the restroom. My teacher permitted me by nodding.

The minute I walked out; I ran upstairs looking for my sister's class. There was a small rectangular piece of glass above the door handles that allowed me to peek through to find her class. Mimi could see me outside one of the doors I peeked through. Her teacher, a nun, could see Mimi was distracted and turned to look in my direction. She saw me standing there then gave my sister permission to go outside to speak to me. I opened the door slowly as my sister walked to the exiting door. The minute she shut the door, I stepped aside for privacy to start crying. I told my sister in Arabic, "I hate my class. I had no idea what to do, nor could I communicate." She calmed me down for as long as she could. The time came when we both knew we had to return to our classes. Even though it was unbearable for me, I had to go back to my class. The ridiculous never-ending circles that the teacher made turned out to be cursive—something I had never seen and later labored to learn.

My teacher, Mrs. Nillo, was from the Philippines. She had a very thick accent. Learning to speak English from her was difficult. When giving us a spelling quiz, she would always say in a very thick accent, "I will repeat it three times." By the third time she repeated the word, I could barely make out what she was saying.

Mid-year, my teacher started calling on me. I could speak some English. "Nadia, what is three times three?" I stood up from my seat as required, translated the equation into Arabic, solved the math problem, then translated it back into English. The minute I was ready to give her my answer, in a harsh, impatient voice, Mrs. Nillo would say, "Sit down." Looking back, I am surprised that she was not more sympathetic to me. English was her second language.

During recess, my classmates would surround me, asking me to repeat English words unfamiliar to me. The nun would walk over; judging from her facial expression, I guessed the students were asking me to repeat inappropriate words that sounded funny with my thick Iraqi accent.

Fortunately, when I was in Potomac, Maryland, my Aunt Mary Grace took us to church. Going there introduced me to the Catholic ritual of receiving Communion. It was made clear to me that I was not allowed to participate in Communion at my Catholic school because I was not baptized. I learned the Lord's Prayer at the school's church. Sitting in the back at the last pew, feeling singled out, made me feel different, unaccepted. I was the only person not allowed to participate. I could not understand why they wouldn't let me join them to receive Communion. After all, my mother was Catholic. In the Middle East, my teachers knew we celebrated the Christian holidays. I was still required to memorize and participate in Muslim prayers. Never was I forbidden to participate in my religious practice. I did not understand the logic, or the role baptism played in church. In Iraq and Iran, the father's theological orientation identifies the child's practicing religion.

My mother got a job as a jailer at the Oakland police station, quite a departure from an English professor at the Women's University in Tehran. She was determined to make it here without my father's assistance, mostly because she wanted to divorce him without relying on him financially. The seventies was a great period for women's liberation, but it also signified a period in history when more women became economically disadvantaged while fighting for equality and independence.

Walking to school presented some challenges. My sister Mimi, my brother Jamal, and I walked to school and back together. One day shortly after starting Catholic school, for some reason I can't remember, my siblings were not walking with me. On my way home, on the street corner, a young boy was stalking me. He was a few years older than I. I crossed the street when I passed the corner store. The boy jumped out in front of me from the left side to rob me. Unable to speak English, my attempts to communicate in Arabic frustrated him. Once he realized that I was from a different country, he used his hands, gesturing for me to leave.

This was 1969. It turned out we lived in East Oakland on 98th Avenue, a place that was considered the Harlem of the East Bay, during a racially volatile time. I had no idea I was seen as a white person living in a predominately African American neighborhood where the tension between whites and blacks did not go unnoticed. I never understood why, since we are all people living in one area. Arabs come in all shades; my new neighborhood was no different except for the racial tension.

I felt the same racial and cultural tensions for being American in Iraq, and an Iraqi when I lived in Iran. Even though I did not share these American racial feelings, I could not avoid the racial crossfire between the white and black communities.

Shortly after moving to our new home, my mother lost her job as a jailer because she broke the rules at work for giving a prostitute cream for her coffee. Management considered this act unacceptable. The reality is that there was another woman who was jealous of her. She taunted my mother, calling her names daily. Mom came home devastated the day she lost her job. I could feel the weight of her grief, but I did not understand the economic ramifications. She later gained employment at the United States Post Office with an excellent salary and good benefits. She waited six months to ensure her job was secure before she moved us to another city.

In 1970, we moved to Berkeley from Oakland. I attended Lincoln Elementary School, where I thrived. My teacher, Mrs. West, was a beautiful African American woman married to a white man. She was one of the most influential teachers in my life. I loved going to school to learn from her. My grades went from D-minuses at a Catholic school to As in the public school. Mrs. West used to allow us to earn 25 extra credits a week to bring up our grades. I would receive the standard credits plus the 25 additional credits every week. She inspired me and made learning fun, exciting, and creative. I was a sponge for every topic she taught.

One day, when I was walking down the hall during recess, an African American boy came up to me, raised his hand above his head, and said, "Give me five." Still unfamiliar with the colloquial American English language, I responded, "I don't have a nickel." in my thick Arab accent. The boy laughed and told me to raise my hand; he explained that it is a greeting ritual when our hands slap one another.

Fifth grade went by quickly. I spent only half a year in sixth grade before moving on to seventh grade. It made me happy to advance, catching up academically to my age group. Jamal attended Willard Junior High.

Jamal and I were very close growing up. When people asked if we were twins, we always said yes. As young children, before coming to the U.S., we did a lot of things together. Some of our ventures got us in big trouble. I still like to say, with a Cheshire smile on my face, it was Jamal's idea. I was merely adventurous, going along with his next venture.

When I was in seventh grade, Jamal in eighth, we joined the swim team at school. Our coach was fabulous—an Italian woman by the name of Aggie, short for Aggratellis. My life changed when I went from swimming for fun to competing, learning to swim all four strokes. My favorite competition was the individual medley.

On the day of the swim meet, our coach would tell us which lane we were competing in. When my event was ready, I would get on the block, a short diving board to place my feet on while bending over. Leaning down on the block, waiting for the gunfire, I would stare at the calm water ahead. My heart was racing, adrenaline spiking, all in anticipation of getting the lead the minute I hit the water. It was challenging to keep a lead in a race once the distance grew to half a lane. When I breathed while swimming, I would check on my competition with my peripheral vision to see how far ahead they were of me. Often, viewing them too far away would discourage me. But one thing always held true, no matter how far away I was from the lead, I had to believe I could catch up, be the fastest swimmer.

I will never forget my first competition; I did not have the right swimsuit. I placed sixth with the slowest time. I could see I was the only person in the pool while my swim mates had long finished the event. Fortunately, I wasn't discouraged. I knew that everyone on my team had more experience than I did. Once I caught up with my teammates' athletic abilities, I slowly started placing second or third, especially in the butterfly events. I was the second strongest swimmer on the team for this stroke, which helped me a great deal when competing in the individual medley event that started with the butterfly stroke, then backstroke, followed by breaststroke, and finished with freestyle. My confidence in this event came from my ability to swim butterfly. At the start of the race, I could gain a lead on the swimmers in the other five lanes. Other swimmers also had their best stroke, which gave them confidence in catching up if they fell behind in the beginning.

Swimming the butterfly stroke made me feel powerful. To this day, I can see the fabulous, young, African American teenager who taught us how to swim the butterfly in seventh grade. She had the grace of a dolphin, making the stroke look so easy; I tried to imitate her, quickly realizing how difficult it was.

During lunchtime in middle school, there was palpable racial tension. Again, I did not understand it, but I could feel it. One day, during lunch, while sitting on a square wooden bench that circled a tree, an African American girl walked down to slap every white girl sitting on the bench. When she approached me, I looked up at her and heard her friend say, "No, that's Jamal's sister," catching her friend's hand in mid-motion. My racial slap was avoided, but the next white girl was not forgiven. Surprised by a sudden hit in the face, she sat motionless in shock, reconciling what had just happened to her.

Berkeley in the early seventies was a political hotbed. It was still building on the University of Berkeley 1964 "Student Free Speech" movement. The political climate was influenced by the civil rights and anti-war sentiments, raising the special interest groups' demands for equality. The Women's Movement, the Black Movement, the Disability Movement, and the Gay Liberation Movement gave a voice to a group of people who were no longer willing to suffer in silence. This historical rise in pop-culture influenced the American lifestyle in permanent ways.

When my mother drove me to middle school on Telegraph Street, I saw a car dealership with small vehicles turned over. There were plumes of tear gas with law enforcement teams wearing gas masks. The armed policeman chased rioters.

"Mom, why are those people wearing masks. Why are the other people running? Why are the people in uniform with bats in hand chasing people?" I asked. I can't recall my mother's answer. I do remember that she stayed calm, answering with no inflection in her voice, making it seem like a passing event. Her response could have come from having lived in the Middle East where national guards raided our home, arrested my father, and enforced curfew hours that exposed us to witnessing brutal deaths. Whatever was in front of us on Telegraph near the University of Berkeley was not as bad as what she had already experienced.

Jamal graduated from eighth grade, moving on to West Campus. All the eighth-grade graduating Berkeley students from different public schools went to West Campus for one year before attending Berkeley High. Eighth grade marked the second time my brother Jamal and I attended different schools than our other siblings. Knowing that my brother was there for me in case I needed him, gave me solace.

My academic English classes confused me. Usually, students are enrolled in one English class every year. For some reason, the administration enrolled me in two English classes. One was a "remedial English" class; the second was a "high potential" English class. I did not understand why they placed me in the most advanced and least advanced English classes at the same time. I loved my advanced English class. We read iconic books like "Lord of the Flies" with homework requiring us to reflect on their meaning by writing book reports. Listening to other students' opinions in class made it the most exciting course of all. It was a dynamic, interactive experience.

On the first day of my remedial English class, I went to my assigned room; no one was there. I sat down, waiting for the teacher. Then a second student walked in. We sat there quietly for a while; the teacher never arrived. We introduced ourselves to one another. Interesting enough, Margit was from Germany. Her father was a visiting physicist, a professor from the University of Munich who took a one-year sabbatical at the University of Berkeley. Our English remedial class turned out to be a self-paced class based on an honor system. We did our in-class assignments together, which helped both of us. I had no idea back then that this fortuitous meeting would be a lifetime friendship.

Margit was a natural athlete. She excelled in everything she did. As I ran around the bases after hitting the softball deep in the right outfield, Margit frustrated me by catching it. Yet she was unassuming and humble, making it easy to be friends. One of our most memorable events that year, before Margit moved back to Germany, was a one-week Girl Scout hiking, backpacking, and camping trip to Yosemite. As expected, Margit's stamina kept her in front of the group. We had several base camps that had magnificent views. We loved being on an adventure together. Lying on rocks, jumping into lakes on a hot summer day after a long hike, was heavenly. We learned to travel light, eat what was available, hand wash clothes, and play the card game "hearts" for hours.

On the last day of the trip, we walked through a magnificent flat field of blooming flowers. It was as if they were there cheering us on the final leg of our journey. It was a beautiful summer ending for two 13-year-old girls, originally from foreign countries, who called Berkeley home.

Catholic School class photo

Margit and I in Yosemite

Yosemite overlook

Jamal and I showing off our swim team ribbons

my protector Jamal

Chapter 3
My Epic Teenage Trip to Europe

Margit's departure to Germany was a new milestone for me. My only friend from school who could relate to my circumstances went home to resume her life. The one thing I discovered about being bicultural is that I never felt fully immersed in one culture. I had become a hybrid of both cultures.

Like Jamal, it was my turn to attend West Campus before attending Berkeley High. This year was different. I had a tribe of friends who knew me from elementary school, a thick-accented foreign girl who had developed into a Californian teenager.

Margit and I wrote many letters to one another. Even though I had good friends, I missed her. She was like a sister to me. I enjoyed teaching her the cultural nuances that come with the territory when one moves to a different country, like what "give me five" means.

In 1974, Margit's family invited me to stay with them in Germany. My mother was open to letting her 15-year-old daughter travel to Europe by herself. Over the year, we discussed and planned my trip there. I left school a bit early that year, departing the first week of June with my first stopover at my Aunt Mary Grace's home in Potomac, Maryland.

Five years had elapsed since our earlier arrival in 1969. I was looking forward to going back to visit my family. My cousin Margaret was closest in age to me. I loved her. We spent the early weeks of summer together, participating in art and swim team at the club down the street.

The day before I left my cousin's home, my aunt took us all to Wolf Trap Farm National Park for the Performing Arts in Virginia for the 4th of July. It was landscaped beautifully with foliage, flowers, and green manicured lawns that never seemed to end. Bands were playing in different parts of the park. It was an all-day festival.

Before the fireworks show, we all went to look for a place to sit down on the lawn in front of the firework machine. The closest we could get was about two to three hundred feet away. When the fireworks started, we were mesmerized by the endless varying light shapes; it felt terrific sitting there on a warm night watching different patterns of light grace the sky. Then, suddenly, people from the front rows stood up and started running back towards our direction. A stampede of people headed our way. In shock, I sat there, unable to process what was going on. My cousin David grabbed my left arm from the back to pull me up as he stood to run in the same direction the crowd was moving in. The evening ended with helicopters, emergency vehicles, the fire department, and local television stations that came to report on the unfortunate event. The firework machine had malfunctioned. It started to shoot the fireworks toward the people who were sitting on the front of the lawn. In self-preservation, the mob stood up and ran away from the fire.

At first, the calm, beautiful evening appeared to be a wonderful ending to my month. I felt peaceful gazing at the sky, imagining what Europe would be like. Unfortunately, the surreal nightmare that ensued with people screaming, crying, running in horror to protect themselves and their loved ones, has had a lifelong effect on me. Ever since that fateful day, I never have been a big fan of fireworks, especially up close.

My stay ended on July 5. Aunt Mary Grace drove me to the airport to catch my flight to Luxembourg. I took giant steps to board my plane. I felt excited to meet up with Margit and experience her life in Germany, feeling restless in anticipation of the journey ahead of me.

I arrived in Luxembourg on a warm, sunny day, a beautiful small country landlocked between France, Germany, and Belgium. While collecting my belongings at the airport, I spoke to several people, inquiring about directions to the youth hostel downtown. To my relief, they gave me instructions in English. I caught a bus to downtown Luxembourg, then walked with one piece of luggage, thinking this was my first European trip without my immediate family. Checking in, I showed my youth hostel I.D. card. The person at the desk asked me if I had the thin silk-like lining required for the beds. I said yes. The mandatory insert is meant to keep the bedding clean. A traveler is only supposed to sleep in the shell lining of the bed. I paid my fee for the next few nights. The desk clerk gave me a schedule for the evening events, which included a disco night.

It was July 6, 1974. I walked downstairs a few hours after dinner to a dark room in the basement with loud familiar music. The strobe lights contributed to the festive ambiance, with the pretense of being at a nightclub. At first glance, I could see a few people dancing. Most of the guests stood against a cement wall introducing themselves to one another. I met a few Australians and Canadians who I later went sightseeing with.

The desk clerks at the youth hostel and everyone I encountered spoke English; it gave me the false impression that catching a train to Munich later that week would be easy. Every day upon awakening, I went to the museums and historical sites of interest, as instructed by my mother. I mostly spent time alone except for taking in a few sights with the Canadians and Australians. They were my favorite tourist to explore the city with. Their kicked-back, relaxed, never-overreacting disposition to any circumstance, made them the ideal tourists. I avoided loud Americans to demonstrate that we are not alike.

Getting a direct train to Germany was difficult. I met two German girls at the youth hostel who were being picked up by their parents. They invited me to spend one night at their home to help me get to the train station the next day.

After my hosts' parent dropped me off in Stuttgart to catch the Deutsche Bahn, late in the afternoon, I walked to the teller's window to purchase a ticket. Opening my passports with a signed traveler's check, I slipped my documentation on the counter under the window. A woman reached out, looked at me to verify my identity from my passport photo, took the traveler's check from Bank of America, and pulled out a very thick binder with plastic sleeves with copies of traveler's checks from around the world. She thumbed through the book once, then again, but she could not find a copy from my issuing bank to verify it as an acceptable currency exchange. It was getting late; the train station was closing. I had no idea what to do next. This circumstance presented a surprise that neither my mother nor I had anticipated or planned for.

To help me, the clerk at the desk called the American military to pick me up. A nice young man came to the train station; he greeted me in the ticket area. I explained that my traveler's checks were not accepted as a viable currency to purchase a ticket to Munich. He comforted me by saying, "I understand, but the train station is closing. You will have to return tomorrow to purchase a ticket." He offered to host me at his house for the evening. Reticent to accept his offer, he read my mind. "I am a married man. You can come home with me and sleep on the couch until tomorrow morning. I will bring you back to the train station and help you get your ticket to Munich." His honest demeanor felt warm and caring. In his eyes, I could see that he wanted to help me—a 15-year-old stranded teenager in a foreign country. I took him up on his offer. Everything played out as he described it. The next day, he took me back to the train station, helped me purchase my ticket, then bid me farewell.

This was one of the few times I had ever been on a train by myself apart from BART, the subway in Berkeley that connected some of the neighboring cities in the San Francisco Bay Area. The Deutsche Bahn moved at high speed; I liked the freedom I felt. It reminded me of the first time I walked down the street to the store in Iran to buy pistachios.

I wasn't scared or uncertain. I was on an adventure meeting up with my best friend, Margit.

After arriving at the Munich train station, I needed to find my way to a suburb, a little town named Baldham. Inexperienced with my transportation options, I took the most expensive route and caught a taxi to my friend's home. The cab driver took advantage of me. Driving on the freeway, he stayed behind the slowest car in the middle of the highway, even though the other lanes were open for him to pass the slow vehicle in front of us. The meter made me anxious. I was concerned about running out of money. My currency was limited. It did not occur to me to go to the bank first to cash in more of my traveler's checks before hailing a cab.

Once the meter hit the exact amount of money in my wallet, I asked the taxi driver to pull over to drop me off. Feeling discouraged by my currency exchange experience at the Stuttgart train station, walking to my friend's home felt like the better option. With heavy luggage in hand, I had to keep switching arms to regain the feeling in my numb hand.

The distance to my destination was unknown. Everything looked the same to me. No really distinguishing architectural features on the exterior of the houses made me wonder if I was walking in circles. By God's grace, I finally found Margit's home. I rang the doorbell, Mrs. Sussman opened the door to greet me. I was so happy to see her. She always made me feel welcome. A large guest room was prepared for me downstairs. It was bigger than Margit's room upstairs.

Margit was still in school while I settled in and waited for her. My mother gave me a pound of coffee from Pete's to give Mrs. Sussman as a gift. The roasted coffee was a specialty item from Berkeley. Pete was from Holland. His father roasted coffee there. He introduced gourmet roasted bean coffee in Berkeley during the 1960s, before becoming popular in the rest of the U.S.

When Margit finally got home, we were very excited to see each other and catch up. Now I could finally meet the people she wrote to me about. The next day, I had permission to attend Margit's last day of school. She wrote to me about a boy she liked. I was looking forward to meeting the young man who had her teenage heart. Attending her German school was fun. Many of the students spoke English. I met her new boyfriend and friends. They were intelligent, interesting to talk to. This year was an important year for them. They had to decide if they were on the university track or going to trade school.

Margit's year in ninth grade ended with a field trip to the Alps. As a guest, I could join her class. We took a train to the mountains, hiking great distance to check into a Chalet. It was then that I realized why Margit's hiking in Yosemite was so effortless for her. The students in Germany were accustomed to taking long hikes, climbing rocks in the Alps to reach their destination. One of the few hiking trips I took was with Margit to Yosemite. I was the slowest in the group then and the slowest now. Leaders periodically fell back to check up on me. When this happened, I knew they wanted to ensure I was walking in the right direction before they got too far ahead.

The Chalet was big. It housed all the attending 15-year-olds. After a long hike, we were all sitting and relaxing in different parts of the Chalet. Some of Margit's classmates took an interest in me. As in my days on the playground in the Catholic school, the German boys in the Chalet asked me to read German words out loud from a publication. I did not see any offensive images, agreeing to test my German. They laughed, howling when I struggled to pronounce some of the words. Margit walked over to see why everyone was laughing so hard. The boys had me reading inappropriate words. The laughter was in response to my elongated pronunciation coupled with a thick American accent. No doubt, they were thoroughly entertained until Margit put a stop to it.

After school had been out for a while, Margit and I decided to cycle to Innsbruck, Austria, from Baldham. It was a 180-mile round trip ride from her home. There was a lake she wanted us to go to that had an island in the middle. With her mother's approval, we packed our two bicycles, starting on a new adventure. Margit's bike had three gears. My bike had one working gear, first gear. We cycled through the rolling Bavarian hillside, passing quaint little towns, I couldn't help but think of the Grimm fairy tales. The illustrations in the children's books resembled Bavaria. Margit stopped to take a break from cycling only to discover that our money for the trip disappeared. This was the first leg of our journey. Neither one us wanted to turn back because of the lack of funds. We stayed on course to our destination.

The strawberries in open fields quenched our hunger. After arriving at the lake, we realized we forgot the paddles for the blow-up boat. We jumped into the water once we inflated it with our breath, taking turns, pulling it to the island. The water was soothing, cooling my body after cycling for hours. We spent the day frolicking in the water. With a late start, we began to make our way back home. Halfway through the trip, hungry and tired from swimming all day, we decided to approach a farm to seek accommodations. Margit was too embarrassed to ask for help. I spoke the little German I knew to ask if we could spend the night, coupled with hand gestures, explaining to the farmers that my friend was American and she did not speak German.

The friendly family allowed us to stay with them for one night. They escorted us to their pristine and orderly barn without any bedding. It was a large two-story building that housed hundreds of haystacks for the farm animals. After entering, we climbed the staircase to the loft, and lay down on the hay from exhaustion using our deflated boat as a blanket. There was an open window where a young man surprised us by suddenly appearing from nowhere. He smiled and started to ask me questions about our trip. My German language skills were dismal. Once he realized this, he only stayed for a few minutes before leaving. His departure was a relief to me.

Morning came quickly. The rooster started crowing early. We woke up, brushed the hay off our clothes and hair, and folded our blanket—the deflated boat—placing it on the back of my bicycle. We got ready to leave when the hosting family invited us for breakfast. The invitation delighted me. The last meal we had before making it to the lake was strawberries from a field. Breakfast was freshly baked bread, eggs from the farm's chickens, and milk from their cows. Margit was conservative with her appetite. I wasn't sure if she felt like an imposition. I ate as much as they put on my plate, knowing that we could not anticipate when our next meal would come.

The time came to hit the road. We thanked our hosts for taking us in for the night and providing such a delicious breakfast. I knew the ride home was going to be more difficult than the ride over. Lots of uphill roads in the first gear would be challenging. We still had 60 miles of rolling hills through quaint Bavarian towns before we would reach Baldham. Admittedly, I was not looking forward to cycling uphill with my one gear bicycle. During our ride back home, Margit got so far ahead of me I could not see her. Frustrated, jealous that she had a three-speed, a faster bicycle than mine, I pulled off the two-car lane road, and with the loudest voice I could muster, I screamed her name. "Mar-git!! Mar-git! Mar-git!" I just got angrier and angrier because I did not know which direction I should go in. By the time she came into sight, I had already released all the tension from my body from screaming her name in rage. It was therapeutic. My anger dissipated into relief when she cycled up to me. We finally made it home, excited about showering, wearing clean clothes, and having dinner with the family. I don't recollect if Mrs. Sussman was irked with us, nor am I sure if we shared all the details on our cycling trip with her.

My time in Munich came to an end. I left my luggage at Margit's home, purchased a backpack and sleeping bag, and then activated my Eurail pass to board a train to Copenhagen. Sitting on the train before our departure, I couldn't help but relive my adventures with Margit. Some of the conversations, the memories, made me smile. To mask my happy feelings from the people sharing my compartment, I looked out the window to the scenery, turning my head, facing away from the passengers across from me, pretending to yawn.

Copenhagen was small compared to Munich. A statue, "The Little Mermaid," sat on a rock near the waterway looking into the distance. This famous statue is based on Hans Christian Andersen's children's story. Disney turned his book into "The Little Mermaid" movie.

At night, lying in bed in Copenhagen, thumbing through my international travel guide, I found a ship from the 1900s that served as a youth hostel for travelers in Stockholm. Excited about sleeping on a historic boat, I caught a train to Sweden, checking in on the ship. Although my room was a two-person bunk bed cabin, it was fall. There were very few European travelers, with schools back in session. The Swedish people I encountered were always helpful when I needed instructions. Sometimes, they would walk me to my destination.

One night I decided to go to the movies. The only American movie playing at the time was "The Exorcist." I sat in the theater, watching, terrified in the dark, fearing having to go back to the ship, to my empty room with the lights turned off per house rules. After returning, I laid in my bunk bed, anxious, tossing, turning, fighting flashbacks from the film's terrifying scenes. I was freaked out and couldn't wait for the breaking of dawn to sit in the rejuvenating sunlight. That morning was sweeter than most. I felt a new sense of revival when I woke up.

Walking in Stockholm, I met a Christian man who wanted me to accept Jesus Christ as my Savior. Feeling vulnerable after seeing "The

Exorcist," I saw no harm in discussing religion or accepting Jesus Christ as my Savior. The man walked me to the Gamla Stan pier after the sunset, a beautiful medieval neighborhood with cobblestones and preserved historic buildings, to participate in a ritual. We stood apart, holding our hands arms-length apart. He said, "Repeat after me, I accept Jesus Christ as my Savior." I repeated his words; then, we parted ways.

Before leaving, he asked me to join him in a Christian community outside of Stockholm. I told him I would think about it. He scribbled the address on a piece of paper and handed it to me, hoping his offer would be accepted. The next day, I gave considerable thought about joining his Christian community as I stood at the platform at the train station.

I boarded a train to go north to Oslo, Norway. The temperature was dropping; I was colder than usual. After taking in the beautiful icy fjords, a stunning mountain range, I headed south, working my way back to Munich. The first stop was Amsterdam. It began to rain when my train pulled up into the station. Failing to secure accommodations at the youth hostels, I decided that this would be a one-day trip. Even though I usually carried three to five hundred dollars on me at a time, it did not occur to me to go to a hotel when the hostels were full. I took my mother's instructions literally: "Nadia, when you arrive in a new city, go to the youth hostel first to check in, drop off your luggage, visit all the historical sites, and send me postcards. If you need money, write to me in advance. Let me know where you will be. I will send you my letters airmail and wire money to the American Express office for you to pick up."

My mother certainly had a lot of confidence in me. I didn't think much about traveling alone because she mapped out my activities about what to do when arriving in a new city. I followed her orders literally with very few deviations.

I walked around Amsterdam for a while, undecided about what to do. I saw many women in shorts skirts standing in the cold rainy streets near the train station and felt sorry for them, believing they were poor, without money to buy longer warmer clothes. Walking through the city with my backpack, I ended up along a canal. It was in the red-light district, a legal prostitution neighborhood with women sitting near their living room windows with a large piece of paper taped to it from the inside. The dark evening got colder; I decided to leave Amsterdam after taking shelter in a few churches.

Going back to Munich solo was much easier the second time around. I arrived back in early September after being away for three weeks. Margit's home was now my European home base. After feeling weary from traveling, I would return there to rejuvenate before leaving on my next trip.

A good friend's mother had an old friend she wanted me to meet in France. I agreed to visit her. The train station in Paris was beautiful, much larger than I anticipated. I disembarked in wonderment, looking up at the beautiful ceiling, admiring the architecture around me. A man dressed in a three-piece grey suit with a hard-black briefcase, grabbed me by my privates as I passed by. Enraged by his act, I walked quickly to catch up with him. With one hand, I slugged him as hard as I could, hitting the arm that was holding his briefcase. He muffled his pain while jerking his body, quickly walking away from me.

After leaving the train station, I was given directions to which bus I should take to my host's home. I paid my fare and sat down on the first seat on the right side of the bus across the street from the train station, as instructed by the attendants. This way, I could keep an eye on my stop. No one was on the bus except me. After I spent a few minutes sitting quietly in the empty bus, the driver locked the doors, left his seat, and came to sit next to me, and said, "I, I, love you, compre compre?" I shook my head, no, looking out the window to mark my disinterest in the conversation. He kept on for five minutes until his break was over.

Fortunately, the driver was not malicious. He could have made my trip more difficult for rudely rejecting his overtures, bypassing my stop without telling me. I found my friend's home. Her house was in Saint-Cloud, a suburb of Paris. She was an older woman, an excellent host who took it upon herself to ensure that I experienced the Eiffel Tower and excellent food. My host offered me wine with meals, never giving up during lunch or dinner. She would ask, "Nadia, would you like a glass of wine?" Declining politely every time, I was hoping she would stop asking me. Eventually, I gave in, feeling that it was an important cultural ritual for her that she wanted me to experience.

Taking the standing room only Metro to the Louvre, men took advantage of women by standing close to them. They pushed their body to rub their crotch against a woman's body. I moved around the train whenever this happened to me.

After exiting the station, I entered the Louvre, paid my entrance fee, got a map, and went looking for Leonardo da Vinci's Mona Lisa, per Mother's instructions. Surprised by the small size of the painting, I had to make my way through the crowd to get a closer look. I leaned in to observe her famous smile. She looked sad to me.

I was impressed with the marvelous collection of artworks at the Louvre. It captivated me. Walking for hours at a time, no matter how exhausted I was, I couldn't force myself to leave. In an inexplicable way, my trip to the Louvre cemented me to the European culture. I discovered Monet, Manet, Cezanne, Degas, Botticelli, Dali, Matisse, Pissarro, Gauguin, Renoir, and Rodin.

I sat at a café after the museum closed, drank a cappuccino, smoking Gauloises cigarettes. It made me feel European, adult-like. I dreaded taking the Metro back. Paris's mass transportation painted a different, unsafe picture for young women in a city admired for its art and recognized for its romance. The second time on the Metro, I pushed men back. Later, I wore a backpack to keep them at a distance.

Tired to plan my next destination, I decided to go to the train station in Paris, open my map, and close my eyes, letting fate select my next destination by going to the city my index finger randomly pointed to. Madrid, Spain, it is. Given my departure time, catching a direct train to Madrid was not possible. I needed to find a connecting train in the South somewhere. But there was no way I could make the connecting train. Impulsively, I decided to travel as far south as I could, then hitchhike to Madrid.

I don't remember which train station I stopped at before looking for a location to hitchhike. Luckily, not too far from the station, I saw a man riding in the direction I was going. We stood there for a long time with our thumbs out; no one stopped. I had an idea. I used to love black and white movies from the '30s and '40s. "San Francisco" came to mind, with Clark Gable and Jeanette MacDonald. The film is based on the 1906 San Francisco earthquake. There is a scene in the movie where Clark Gable and Jeanette McDonald are hitchhiking. Frustrated with the cars that kept passing, Jeanette MacDonald suggested to Clark Gable to hide in the bushes when she stuck out her thumb for a ride. Within minutes, after Clark Gable disappears, a car stopped to pick her up. With his signature mischievous smile, Clark Gable jumps in the back of the vehicle after Jeanette McDonald gets in.

I decided to borrow the scene from the movie. Standing there together for at least an hour, we ascertained that we both were going to Madrid. I asked the man, whom I had a limited conversation with, if he would hide in the bushes with our luggage, allowing me to hitchhike alone. He agreed. Just like the movies, a big truck stopped. I spoke to the driver to let him know there were two of us; he was OK with the extra person. I motioned my acquaintance from afar with hand gestures in the dark to come out of the foliage, and he got into the big truck as we made our way down to Madrid.

Southern Europe was much warmer, even when it rained. I visited the National Museum in Madrid and was introduced to Rubens, Goya, and Rafael's artwork. I saw a bullfight and flamenco dancers. I took a trip on a small, one-car train to Segovia, an ancient city north of Madrid with an aqueduct built in the first century by the Romans. I loved walking around, imagining what life must have been like during this time. I decided to catch a train to Barcelona, arriving at dusk. The youth hostel was challenging to find. I stopped a woman to ask her for directions. She informed me that Barcelona only had a youth hostel for men. She invited me to spend a couple of nights at her house. She seemed trustworthy. Before we left our meeting location, she said, "I need to stop at a bookstore before we go to my place," I told her it would be fine. She walked over to her motorcycle. I got on the back. She waited for me to balance my heavy backpack before she drove off.

The bookstore was quiet—few people were there. Meandering around, I looked at the displayed books, curious as to what locals viewed as appealing. My new acquaintance was out of sight. I did not pay attention to her until she was ready to leave. She lived near the bookstore. When we arrived at her home, she pulled out two beautiful, large coffee table books. I did not see her pay for them and asked when she purchased them. "I stole them and put them in my backpack," she said. Her answer surprised me, making me feel uncomfortable. The next day, I visited the seaside in Barcelona, sitting at a cafe people watching. The sea air was refreshing. Although I love the ocean, I am not much of a beachgoer.

Thumbing through my travel book in Barcelona, I saw a picture of a statue in Lisbon. It was the "Sanctuary of Christ the King" built in May 1959. It caught my interest. It was a giant statue of Christ with open arms that stood 82 feet tall and 25 feet wide. I was excited to explore Portugal as I disembarked at the Lisbon train station. Walking downtown, I could hear loud voices coming from a large crowd ahead, wondering if there was a special event or religious holiday. Interested in my new surroundings, I met up with the group. Shortly after blending in, I realized I was in the middle of what felt like a revolution, walking with protesters where civil unrest was at its peak.

Strong emotions were being expressed in Portuguese. It was September 24, 1974, the day before a military coup took place. It marked the end of the Estado Novo (New State), when authoritarian rule was dominated by civil unrest and a military coup after 48 years. My arrival in Portugal was one of the worst possible times for any tourist. The chaos on the streets with standing guards made me feel unsafe. I struggled with what to do next. Should I stay, let the chaos quiet down, then go to the Sanctuary of Christ the King? Or leave? Impulsively, I headed back to the train station, feeling more at ease as the echoing unrest started to fade. I met people there who were also visiting from Berkeley. Like me, they too were leaving.

I took a train to Madrid from Lisbon and hopped on an express train to southern Spain. I decided to go to Morocco since the people there spoke Arabic. First, I needed to get to Tarifa to catch a ferry to Ceuta Morocco, a popular beach town among the British. Delighted to be out of the political chaos, I boarded a train in Spain, placed my backpack on the rack above my seat, and sat down before the train departed. Two British women sat across from me. Tired from my travels, my senses were heightened, taking note of the details of my surroundings. The train slowly started to move; the conductor leaned out of the door to ensure no one else was boarding while the train was in motion. Once underway, the doors were shut, then locked. Some of the passengers rolled down their windows, waving to loved ones. Witnessing their tears as they said their goodbyes was touching. As the train lost sight of the station, the mournful passengers sat motionlessly, hanging on to their last visual memory of their loved ones. I sat there, wondering if these people were leaving family and friends forever. I was hoping that their sadness would dissolve with their new port of destination.

The British women sharing the compartment with me said they were heading to Morocco, "a beachy environment to develop beautiful tans." A few hours into the ride, the train came to a halt. We sat there for a while with no news as to when the train would start up again. The compartment started getting hot. One of the British women, Ann, wanted to go to the snack bar but was scared because of the Moroccan soldiers. I volunteered to go and pick up the drinks for us.

Entering the cafeteria compartment was blinding. It was filled with thick cigarette smoke. Some of the soldiers wanted my attention. I ignored them, making my way to the counter. They were irritated with my dismissal of their catcalls. Feeling unsafe, I slowly started backing up when four drunken men lunged towards me. I went to exit. The sliding doors were heavy, making it difficult to leave quickly. The soldiers started to follow me. Their pace picked up with mine. I began to run, wrestling heavy doors from one compartment to another. Looking up, I saw two drunken soldiers heading towards me. They must have exited the train since it was stopped, running to the compartment ahead. This way, they could box me in. With two men behind me and two in front, instinctively I ran to the left, opened the bathroom door, and closed it as quickly as possible, pushing my body against it.

With sweaty palms, I struggled to lock the door. One soldier started to push against it. I used my weight to lean into the door with all my might, forcing it to shut. My hands shook when I latched the door. I sat on the toilet with the seat down, petrified, unsure what my next move would be.

The train was still at a halt. I buried my face in my hands, confused, scared. I slowly looked up towards the window to see a soldier, struggling to pull the window down from the outside. I jumped up, went to the window, and pushed it up as he was pulling it down. Struggling again, with all the force I could muster, I was able to lock the window. I went back, sat on the toilet seat, wondering how this nightmare was going to end.

I heard a noise below me. I lifted the toilet seat cover, curious if the sound came from outside. There was a man's face at the bottom. One of the soldiers lay there on the train track with his head at the bottom of the toilet, laughing, taunting me. In fright, I shut the lid, flushed the toilet, sat there for hours, swaying my body, praying, scared. Once the drunken soldiers were quiet for an extended time, I waited even longer to ensure that it was not a trap.

A lot of time had passed when I rallied the courage to leave my shelter. I took a deep breath, slowly unlocking the bathroom door. One soldier lay there on the train floor, sound asleep, guarding the bathroom door. I stepped over him in slow motion, looked back, walked past him, and then looked to my left and right to make sure I was safe again. The train walkway appeared to be clear; I ran to my compartment.

The British girls left me a note, thanking me and letting me know that they were at the snack bar. Traumatized by the soldiers, I sat down speechless, with no explanation for my acquaintances after they came back as to why it took me so long to return empty-handed.

I arrived at the Tarifa port early the next morning. Waiting in line, I met two Moroccan men. One was an engineer, the other a professional actor. After boarding the ferry to Northern Africa, the men invited me to join them for a drink. I had water; one of them had an alcoholic beverage, the other ordered a Coca Cola. We sat enjoying the breeze as the ferry took off. The three of us were having a lively conversation. Suddenly, the authorities approached our table to handcuffed the engineer. They took him away. Shocked by the sudden arrest, I didn't move. I felt uncertain as to what had just transpired. When we arrived in Morocco, the man was released. I asked him why he was arrested. "Muslims are not supposed to drink alcoholic beverages during holy holidays," he said. This day also happened to be holy.

I grabbed my backpack, making my way to the exit. The two men asked me where I was staying. I told them I had not decided yet. They told me they were staying at a beautiful place on the beach nearby. I decided I would stay there, rent a room, and explore the town. As I walked off the ship, a man on a bicycle asked me if I was American. I said, "Yes." He asked me if I was traveling with people I knew. I said, "No." He begged me not to go with these two strange men. He told me it was dangerous for women to go to Morocco by themselves. I told him that I spoke Arabic, letting him know I understood the language; navigating around town would not be difficult for me. Furthermore, I knew the culture.

Young children standing on the street greeted us when we were walking down a metal ramp. They spoke four different languages. They asked us if we spoke English, German, French, or Spanish. It was impressive. The young boys created a business for themselves by engaging passengers to sell their goods when disembarking. They preyed on our Western values that children should not work, knowing we would buy from them because we felt sorry for them.

I arrived at the hotel. I was surprised that I could not understand what the desk clerk said when he spoke. It sounded like pidgin Arabic, a dialect that is closer to the Berber language than the classical Arabic that everyone reads and writes.

My two new friends said the hotel only had two rooms left. It seemed like a setup to me. In English, I asked the desk clerk for a room. He confirmed they did not have a vacancy and that my new acquaintances got the last two openings. The engineer said I could share his accommodations. At fifteen years of age, it never occurred to me to request that the men share a room instead. Distrusting the person I need to share a room with, I had decided in advance that I would pull out my sleeping bag and stay fully clothed before turning in for the night. I went up to the assigned room first. A few hours had passed before the engineer met up with me. He walked into the room and was angry, raising his voice, asking me why I did not have on lingerie.

I eclipsed his rampage by screaming at him in Arabic, called him a bastard, the son of a whore. It stopped him in his tracks. He got in bed underneath the covers. I put my sleeping bag on the bed and slept lightly. At sunrise, I quietly gathered my belongings, left the room, and checked into another room.

There was a knock on my door. I didn't open it and asked who it was from the inside of my room. A man responded, "Room service." I told him, "I did not place an order." He said the engineer ordered me breakfast on a silver platter. I told him I did not want it. He said, "You might as well eat breakfast. Otherwise, we have to throw it out." Opening the door slowly, the waiter looked at me with a big smile. His intentions seemed questionable. He put the tray down in the middle of the room and slowly walked towards me as if he were going to grab me. I stood near the open window overlooking the patio below; guests were having breakfast. I told him if he got any closer to me, I would scream. He smiled, daring me, taking one step forward. I scooted closer to the window, looked down at the guests, and opened my mouth to scream. He raised his hands for me to stop, then backed off, left, shutting the door behind him.

I decided to go for a walk through the town to window-shop after taking a long nap, making up for the night before. I slept lightly in case the engineer planned on surprising me. I walked into a store to buy leather goods. Americans came in, asking the price for specific items. The price kept changing depending on which tourist asked. I took my time looking around, hearing the different prices quoted depending on how affluent the customer appeared. The range for the same item that was quoted at ten dollars to one customer was quoted at one hundred dollars for another.

The young man who ran the store seemed nice. We spoke for a while. He invited me to go to a restaurant with him for dinner. I had to eat; I thought, why not share the time with someone in an open restaurant to be safe. I stopped by again at five o'clock to go to dinner with this man. We walked to a restaurant. He took me upstairs. I thought we were entering the second level until he opened a door for us. The restaurant guests, mostly Moroccan families, stared at me as I made my way up to the second floor. Watching them watch me going up the staircase tipped me to stay alert.

I entered a private room with twenty men. One of them had a kilo of hash. I sat down with my acquaintance. He gave me a hash pipe. I passed, giving it to the next person without taking a hit. Feeling uncomfortable, I excused myself. I said I had a terrible headache and needed to get some aspirin and go back to my hotel. These unexpected events seemed endless.

Traveling solo in Morocco became unpleasant. From the Moroccan soldiers on the train to the engineer, I reached a breaking point with the shopkeeper. After two days, I decided to head back to Germany.

Waiting for the bus to take me to the ferry, I met two blond, blue-eyed British men. Understanding them took some concentration. They spoke with a cockney accent. We talked about Moroccan men.

They said they both had the same issue. I asked them how long they had been in Morocco; they said they could not remember. It didn't make sense to me. I asked them where they stayed. They said, "A hash farm." Naively, I told them if they check the stamp in their passport, they will know how long they had been in Morocco. I missed what they were implying with their answers. When the bus came, we all sat together, making our way to the ferry. I felt safe with these two men mostly because I expected them, as Western men with similar values, to be more civilized, respectful of the opposite sex.

The ferry arrived. The three of us boarded the boat together. We shared what little food we had. Once the boat docked in Spain, I felt relief, safe to make my way back to Germany. We lined up with all the travelers waiting to go through customs at the port. There was a long line. The guys told me to follow them. We walked up to a guard who was standing alone near an exit. He did not check our luggage, but he waved us forward with his hand under the counter so that no one could see it. Much later in life, I realized these guys were drug smugglers, using me, an innocent 15-year-old girl as a cover. They made it through without being arrested, back to Europe, carrying heavy backpacks filled with hash. I was meant to be the American distraction, impressing authorities that we were three young travelers going through customs, unacquainted with their existing procedures. The guard held the pretense that we were confused. His hand gesture identified him to the drug traffickers as the paid official. We stopped when trying to exit the building; the same guard waved to the other authorities to let them know he checked us.

The three of us searched for a *pension*, the name used in Spain for accommodations like a youth hostel. As luck would have it, there were only two rooms left in the one place we found. Again, I shared one with one of the men with the same intentions as before; accommodations, not romance, dictated our relationship.

Before going back to Germany, my plans changed. I had one last stop before heading north to Germany—seeing the Coliseum in Rome. Shortly after arriving in Italy late that morning, I walked around with my backpack looking for accommodations. I passed an ancient man. He looked like a relic to me, dressed in a toga with a long grey beard. He pinched my buttocks as I walked by. I turned back to look at him, asking with my body language, "what the hell are you doing?" He looked up at me and started laughing. Feeling disgusted, unsure where to stay, I decided to leave Rome that same day.

I reached my limit with the Southern European men. I got in line at the train station. The teller who was helping me with my ticket kept asking me out. My declining his aggressive gestures frustrated him. I asked for a ticket to Venice. He finally stopped harassing me, gave me my boarding pass, and smiled as I walked away. Looking at the ticket, I only took note of the arrival time, so I would not miss the stop if it was in the middle of the night. I didn't think of looking at my ticket to verify my destination. When the train pulled up in Vienna, it occurred to me that the teller's smile was a vindictive retaliatory act for not returning his overtures. I never made it to Venice that trip.

Going back to Germany, I felt like I was reentering a civilized country where common courtesy and social etiquette is the expected code of conduct from men. What a relief.

A letter from my mother arrived at Margit's while I was exploring the South. Mom wanted me to know that I did not need to come back home; I could attend a boarding school in Europe if I wanted to. "Just pick a school, and I'll wire the funds," she wrote.

Tired of traveling, dealing with uncertain events, navigating the different languages and currencies, looking for accommodations, being responsible for all my meals and safety, began to exhaust me. I wrote to my mother, saying "I miss being home. I want to come back now." My mother wired funds for my airplane ticket from Munich back to the U.S.

Throughout my "on-again-off-again" visits to Germany, Mrs. Sussman introduced me to opera in the park in Munich. From that day forward, I loved opera. She also took me to the museum in Munich. One day, Mr. Sussman left the University to join us. They introduced me to Albrecht Durer's artwork, along with his famous self-portrait. We discussed the Apostles in the paintings. This was the first museum where I had seen a black allegorical figure in a historical painting. I wouldn't see another for decades.

Living in the U.S. from the age of ten to fifteen redefined the place I called home. My Middle Eastern heritage, a culture I once identified with, faded forever. I was excited to land on American soil, home sweet home. The first thing I appreciated about being back in the U.S. was my ability to read and communicate with ease.

My mother picked me up at the San Francisco airport. To make myself unattractive while traveling in Europe, I consciously decided to gain weight so the men would leave me alone. It worked to some degree. Mom, lovingly, did not comment on my weight gain or bring attention to it. I shared my uncensored stories with her. I could see the expressions on her face changing, and I read her body language. She was horrified, thinking, "I paid for my daughter's travels, putting her in harm's way." She was grateful I made it home safely. Never again did she offer to fund my travels unless she was by my side.

I started Berkeley High late that year, mid-October. Walking down the halls looking for my first-period class, some girls would look at me, giving me the body check and whispering. I could hear them say, "She has put on a lot of weight." My European adventure was distilled to a superficial commentary; she is back from Europe and overweight.

my passport photo for Europe

one of my favorite photos with my brother Jamal- can you feel the love?

Cousin Liz and I in D.C. before leaving for Europe

wearing my Wolf Ttrap Farm shirt in Luxembourg

Tivoli Gardens Copenhagen, Denmark

youth hostel in Stockholm Sweden

mom picks me up at SFO airport

FROM BAGHDAD TO BERKELEY

Chapter 4
Berkeley High School

A Tumultuous Time Assimilating Back into An Institution

After brushing off the weight comments from the mean girls in the hallway, I found my first-period class. It was English with Mrs. Sullivan. I took a seat in the back of the class, slowly turning my head, looking at all the other students to see who was there. None of my good friends were in my class.

The English teacher was a beautiful, young, articulate African American woman. Two of my siblings were her former students. My sister was an exemplary student. Jamal, my brother, either got As or Fs on his assignments.

I sat in class, listening to Mrs. Selvin give us instructions. It felt condescending. I was not ready to be in a subservient role as a high school student. I had experienced so much on my own. The class seemed trivial in the scope of life. My posture offended my teacher. Fed up with me, she pulled me out of the course to tell me she found me offensive and hurtful. Clueless about how my behavior impacted her, I changed my disposition by becoming more engaged and participating.

My experience changed even more when Mrs. Selvin introduced me to Haiku poetry. I loved writing poetry. In the evenings I started going to a cafe to listen to a classical guitarist play Andre Segovia's famous piece, "Leyenda." The music stirred my emotions. I ordered a cappuccino, smoked my French cigarette, and allowed my words to find their way on the paper. This new venue was a bridge, an outlet in which I became absorbed. It allowed me to express all of my confusion with a lead pencil.

Even though my grades were decent, they could have been better. My disinterest in academics was reflected in my report card.

In 1976, after finishing my sophomore year, my Uncle Rex passed away. It was a difficult time for my Aunt Miriam. She was suicidal. My mother sent me to stay with her for the summer to take care of her. It was hard to see how broken she was. I had to sleep in her bed with her, to keep an eye on her. With time, she started showing signs of feeling better. We had terrific conversations except for her makeover efforts. She wanted me to straighten my hair, and trade in my cotton t-shirts and 501 jeans for a polyester suit. She was also concerned about keeping me engaged, asking me if I would like to participate in the local junior college's play. I said I would. She invited her friend, the director, to her house; he interviewed me, then told me to sign up for the *Show Boat* production at the junior college.

My first day on stage started with building the set. Over time, the production director needed a project manager. He selected me to be his protégé. He taught me how to read blueprints, provided me with resources in a private workstation, and asked me to design a template for the French balcony railings. My success with this project elevated my status to a supervisory position where I ended up managing young men, older than I was, to build spiral staircases. Before my crew started a project, I reviewed the blueprints, materials, and design with them, requesting that they come to get me if something came up. After long days, we would all go to the bar for a drink. Everyone there was of age; it was assumed I was too.

As we got closer to opening night, the stage crew had to work from 9 am to 2 am. My aunt started accusing me of inappropriate behavior for coming home late. I tried rationally explaining how we needed all hands on deck to ensure the stage was ready for dress rehearsal night. She became verbally abusive, intolerant. Tired of her accusations, I moved out after my cousin came to stay. My stage friend Lynette invited me to stay with her while her parents were on vacation. I had a blast living with her, taking the bus to the college without getting a ride from my aunt. I could not tell my aunt I lived in an African American neighborhood because she shocked me once by using the word "nigger. To my horror, I had no idea she was a racist.

We used to visit my Aunt Miriam and Uncle Rex during the holidays. One year, my loving Aunt Thelma and Uncle John moved to Stockton. I asked Aunt Miriam, "Why aren't Aunt Thelma and Uncle John here?" She replied, "I would never let that nigger in my house." Speechless at her response, I felt horrible for my Aunt Thelma. Every time we drove to Stockton, if my Uncle John and Aunt Thelma were home, we would make a special trip to see them.

My mother had a tough time with Aunt Miriam after I moved out. She called me many names while accusing me of all sorts of things that I had not done. My mother knew she never had to worry about me getting in trouble. I am fiercely independent. My personality was such that I would not put up with verbal abuse.

Show Boat was a magnificent production. The actors had beautiful voices. The last day of the performance was electric. We had a cast party at an actor's home. That night was a lovely, warm evening in San Joaquin Valley. I walked into my acquaintance's house; cast members were milling around, celebrating the end of a fun and demanding musical. The dance room was festive with inviting music, beckoning me to join the celebration. I felt elated, accomplished to be part of a magnificent production.

One of the actors, who I used to try to avoid on stage, was inebriated. After spotting me in the living room from the dance floor, he started screaming my name, professing his love in a desperate loud voice from a distance. Embarrassed, humiliated by his public outburst, I asked him to step outside to the front lawn. He was irrational. Reasoning with him was not going to work. He appeared to have mental health issues. Unequipped with the psychology required to communicate with him effectively, I simply listened without interrupting him until he calmed down. His outburst thwarted my desire to speak to all the actors and stage crew. Uncomfortable with the public drama, I left the party.

Returning to Berkeley High that fall, I made a new friend whose father joined the Sun Myung Moon Unification movement, a religious organization. It tore his family apart. Determined to learn more about the organization, my friend and I decided to become undercover Moonies. The term Moonies is a reference to the cult followers who viewed Sun Myung Moon as the Messiah.

We learned that the organization always approached people on the street in twos. This way, each one always approaches the opposite sex by inviting them to dinner in North Berkeley to learn about the organization. My friend and I went to dinner at a Moonie's house near the northside of the University, pretending to be interested in the organization. Our frequent dinners there revealed that a nurse from the organization was assigned to recruit teenagers from Berkeley High. She was a volunteer. Somehow, money from Berkeley High was being donated to the Moonies. I felt I had to put a stop to this. Sun Myung Moon amassed a fortune with his members' assets. Once people became committed to the organization, they donated all their valuables, including their income, homes, anything of material value.

Appalled by my discovery, I went to the principal's office at Berkeley High to request a meeting. After sharing my newfound information with him in our first meeting, he asked me to substantiate my claim. Giving him details about the nurse's volunteer status and her recruitment efforts, sufficed. Shortly after our discussion, she was dismissed. The school board then put an end to a discretionary fund that unintentionally made its way to the Moonies' coffers.

Concerned by the influence Sun Myung Moon had on a vulnerable population, I was finding my junior year in high school difficult. I did not have the attention required to attend class or turn in assignments. Mrs. Wilson, my history teacher, pulled me aside one day by taking me into the faculty room. She sat me down and said, "Nadia, what is going in your life? You are skipping class, not turning in your assignments." I explained to her that I was consumed with the Moonies, sharing all that I had learned. She understood my unyielding interest in the topic and wanted to constructively direct my undercover work by asking me to lecture my peers on the subject. My time spent away from class and the assignments had a purpose. Her validation for my investigative pursuit made me feel successful even though my grades were less than impressive.

I do not know why, but the day I had to speak about the Moonies in class, I dressed up, wearing a blue and white 1940s vintage dress. It was my favorite fashion style. My thick curly hair twisted on both sides with a ponytail tucked in the back of the two twists. I sat in a highchair next to my teacher's desk, playing with a rubber band, passionately sharing my experience with the Moonies. At first, I was nervous. Once my classmates were more interested in my discovery and how it related to them, I got deeper into the story, explaining the emotional and financial toll it takes on a family when their loved one is recruited. I ended my presentation with how the voluntary nurse at Berkeley High was relieved of her duties after the principal and school board members were alerted to a discretionary fund directed to the Moonie's organization.

Mrs. Wilson was a memorable and influential teacher in my life. Her ability to recognize and value my undercover work in some way validated my self-prescribed curriculum. In asking me to lecture, to share what was of interest to me, my journalistic roots unconsciously seeded themselves.

My English teacher, Mr. Bowman, was a former Jesuit. He taught us the great classics, like the *Iliad* and the works of Shakespeare. We had a special connection after running into each other at the San Francisco Opera when I was sixteen. He seemed to make exceptions for me. Even though I was not his best student, my love of opera allowed him to overlook the little things, like not being prepared when coming to class or taking tests.

My disinterest and lack of full participation in school forced me into summer school if I wanted to graduate on time. I signed up for Black Studies. On the first day of class, I was late. With standing-room only, I hovered near the front door, to the left of the teacher. The lecture was about the white man and his treatment of the black community. It did not take me long to transfer out as the only white student. Even though I did not represent the sentiment of the white man, I felt the pressure, as if I was a symbol of oppression. I took a pottery class instead for the units I needed to make up.

My senior year in high school became even more difficult. I made an appointment at the principal's office to ask him if he would transfer me from Berkeley High to East Campus, where all the troubled youth attended high school. He refused to let me go. He felt I was too bright and wanted me to complete Model School A (M.S.A.), a sub-school at Berkeley High, for students on the college track.

In the second semester of my senior year, I decided to drop out of high school to get a job. Every establishment I applied to work for asked me the same question, "Are you a high school graduate?" When they found out I dropped out, they were not eager to hire me. The reality check forced me to go back to school. It was clear no one would hire me if I did not have a high school diploma. By this time, I had lost too many units to catch up. The only way I could graduate was by receiving work credits. My best friend, Katherine's mother agreed to let me volunteer at the bird rescue shelter, established in Berkeley after the 1971 Standard Oil spill. The organization fostered birds back to health.

Native marine life, threatened by a massive oil spill, required rehabilitation. The shelter continued to take in birds, sometimes transported from different areas, to be nursed back to health before releasing them back to their natural habitat. I worked there every day, cleaning the birds and their poop, and feeding them until they were strong enough to feed themselves. The most challenging part of the job was the smell. The fresh outdoor air from the Bay always felt terrific when I left the bird building.

Graduation day was at the Greek theater in Berkeley. It was a long, arduous journey. My four months in Europe changed me. As a child, I was extremely independent. Traveling as a teenager, fueled by my mother's support, I received a cultural education in geography, art, history, music, and language. Unintentionally, my academic years at Berkeley High were a reflection of my curriculum in Europe. I only studied the topics that were of interest to me. If I was assigned an academic project that required me to research something of no interest, I never completed it. If I chose a project to dedicate myself to, like my travel destinations in Europe, I indulged in the topic as long as possible. This approach to education is intellectually stimulating to me. As a result, I could never assimilate to the high school curriculum; I always struggled to fit into a system that did not fully captivate me. Finally, at graduation, my struggles came to an end.

My father reached out to me before I graduated from Berkeley High, inviting me to come live in Baghdad. When he lived in the U.S., I was academic and athletic. He had no idea about my travels or my battles in high school. The summer I spent in Europe, my mother told him I was staying with Margit in Germany. She told me to tell Mrs. Sussman that, when my father called, to say I was out when I was traveling. Fortunately, she never spoke to him.

During the same time, my grandfather came to the U.S., hoping to reconcile my parents and bring them back to Baghdad. Sorry to have missed his visit, I wanted to meet my grandfather at the Eiffel Tower in Paris on his way back home. I wrote to my mother to tell her where and when to tell my grandfather to meet me. As a mature adult, I now realize he would have been horrified to see me travel with a backpack around Europe. Not only was it undignified for a young lady, but he would have viewed my youth hostel accommodations and the transportation choices I made as being substandard. Although my mother and I never discussed it after my return, I highly doubt she shared the information with him. I sat at the Eiffel tower, feeding pigeons for hours in the afternoon, waiting for my grandfather. Disappointed not to see him, I left after it got dark.

I told my father I would come to Baghdad under the condition that he purchase a round-trip ticket to ensure my return. I did not want to be stuck in a white tower compound where exploration and curiosity are unacceptable. Being American would put me under everyone's microscope. My every move would be watched or calculated by someone else.

Many of my high school American friends came to the airport to see me off. My plane had a layover at JFK in New York to catch a connecting flight to Baghdad. When I disembarked at the airport, the people around me seemed aggressive. I felt pushed by them, forced to walk more quickly than I could. Things were falling out of my arms as I made my way down the staircase. The people behind me were agitated, annoyed when I slowed down to pick up my dropped items. New York did not feel like a friendly place.

I boarded my connecting flight, arriving in Baghdad in the afternoon. Nine years had elapsed since my last visit. When I asked my father what I could bring him from the U.S., he said the *San Francisco Chronicle* sports section. In 1977, it was illegal to bring in magazines or newspapers from other countries. The government controlled all of the media outlets. This way, they could manipulate the political and social narrative. There was no such thing as a free press. Journalists dared not write any critical editorials about the government. If they did, they would be killed or imprisoned.

Arriving at the airport, I could see my father waving from a distance. The guard took my passport, then asked, "What is the purpose of your trip?" "Visiting family," I replied. Distracted by my father, I did not pay attention to the immigration officer after returning my passport. My father stood there with open arms. We hugged. When we left the airport, I smiled, turning my head, looking behind me, I handed him the folded sports section to the *San Francisco Chronicle* from the side. He laughed mischievously, excited to catch up on his favorite sports. Locally, he liked the Giants, 49ers, Raiders, and his non-local team, the Dallas Cowboys.

Three years had passed since I had seen him last. When I visited him at his home in Berkeley, we used to hang out at his house and watch his favorite football and baseball teams. He cooked Middle Eastern food for me to eat while watching the games. He also drove me to the San Francisco School of Ballet for one of my weekly classes or picked me up after swim team for fine dining. We were very close. Once my grandfather's efforts in reuniting my father with my mother failed, he arranged a marriage for him in Baghdad. During his last days in the U.S., we spent a lot of time together. I helped him pick out his clothes, shoes, and new wife's wedding dress.

Adjusting to the time change in Baghdad was difficult. I kept waking up in the middle of the night when everyone was asleep, sitting on the rooftop stargazing for hours—then falling asleep when everyone was up. Dad had Valium that he offered me, hoping I would sleep through the night. I kept increasing the dosage without telling him, hoping to get relief. One day my father came home, insisting I stay awake. Clueless as to what too much Valium would do to my system, I was liberal with my dosing. It turns out that more was not better. Poor Dad—my uneducated desperate efforts to sleep threatened my life. He was panicked at the possibility of losing me.

The next day, Dad took me to see my grandmother, "Bibi". She was a significant person in my life growing up. I had not spoken Arabic in years; Dad needed to translate for me. My father always spoke English with us in the U.S. Bibi, (which translates to grandmother in Arabic), asked me, "Why did you dye your hair dark brown?" I asked Dad to explain puberty to her. I was a redhead last time she saw me.

Bibi loved my mother's gift—five pounds of See's candies. Mom had no idea she had diabetes.

The summer before starting college ended after many fun family reunions. Seeing my aunts and some of my favorite cousins, it felt like no time had elapsed since I last saw them. I enrolled at the University of Baghdad to studied German. The professor, a Christian woman, was married to an Iraqi. Her life reminded me of my younger years growing up in Baghdad, where my mother's friends, foreign women, were married to Arab men.

Attending University was exciting. For many of the men and women, it was the first time they experienced coed classes. The hormones for this select group were raging.

Divorce was not common in the culture. When asked about my mother, I replied, "my parents are divorced." People usually responded with, "You poor thing." I let them know that my parents were happy being divorced.

I had five German classes, one political science class, one English class, and one poetry class. My friendship with Margit influenced my desire to learn German. Our uniforms were grey pants or skirts, white shirts, and a blue blazer. I wore a grey skirt or corduroy grey pants with a wool American Navy Sailor uniform for a top.

On my first day in my political science class, the professor lectured on the United States. "America, land of prostitution, land of unwed mothers. Nadia, how do you compare the two countries?" Knowing Iraq has an authoritarian government, where free speech can land you in a prison cell followed by a sudden disappearance, clearing my throat I answered his question carefully. "Both countries have their pros and cons, professor."

One day, while leaving college, a group of men sitting on the bed of a white truck screamed out at me in Arabic, "It's illegal for you to wear pants," and drove off. I did not know if there was such a law or if it had changed. Since they were the only people who mentioned it, for my safety, I alternated between wearing slacks and skirts until I was clear on the dress code policy. Since the issue never came up again, I resumed wearing what I wanted when I felt safe. I believe these traveling nomads were expressing their personal views. In retrospect, if it were a law, my family would have educated me on what was considered acceptable attire.

I had one good friend at the University who was Turkish, married with a daughter. She and I did everything together. We sat in the girl's room during the break and talked to the other language study students. It was a rectangular room with a u-shaped bench along the wall. Next to it was a bathroom.

One day, we had a mandatory protest to demonstrate Iraq's dissatisfaction with Sadat, the president of Egypt, and his efforts in discussing peace with Israel. Everyone in the University had to participate in the protest. Otherwise, their allegiance to the Iraqi government was questioned. I marched in the demonstration until I could slowly fade away from the crowd to catch a bus back home. By this time, my stepmother, whose age is closer to mine than my father's, was a stereotypical second wife. Unwilling to deal with her raging jealously, I moved out to live with my grandmother, Bibi.

Sitting on the bus on my way home, two men my age sat behind me. During the ride, they talked about me, assuming I did not understand them. "You think she is Russian?" said one guy. "No," said the other, "I think she is American. Look at the color of her hair and blue eyes." This dialogue went on and on. In the Middle East, a woman is not allowed to speak to men. It took a lot of self-discipline not to turn around and say to them in Arabic, "No, I am Iraqi and American."

Arriving home, I blew off steam by angrily mocking the men on the bus, screaming profanities, walking up the spiral staircase to my bedroom on the second floor. Bibi always had a great way of calming me down. She said, "Ir tah he," which means "relax" in Arabic. She laughed at my temper. I loved her. We spent a lot of time together. One day she asked me to dye her hair blonde. "Bibi," I asked, "why dye your hair when you are wearing a hijab? No one can see you anyway."

"I like it," she said. We sat in the sunroom while her hair was drying, sipping our tea. A sudden sandstorm filled the room. The strong, forceful wind kept blowing in. We rushed around the room, struggling to close all the windows.

My cousin, a person I was never close to, invited me to go out to the Melwiyah club. Her uncle, a male, was to escort us. We were all close in age. Feeling nostalgic for my western lifestyle, I accepted her offer. Most of my days in Baghdad were spent going to school, studying, or hanging out with family. Her offer was a departure from my usual activities. The big event on Friday night at the club was playing bingo. Everyone dressed up to attend the event. Some men smoked cigarettes and drank alcohol while marking their bingo cards. Women could smoke only if their husbands permitted it. I desperately wanted a cigarette. That evening my cousin, on several occasions, encouraged me to smoke publicly. I did not trust her, sensing she wanted me to do something that would upset my family. I asked my father later if I had smoked publicly at the club, would that have been OK. He said, "Absolutely not. I am glad you did not."

Bibi was an excellent cook. She made her bread in the oven outside near the chicken coop, pickled cucumbers, and baked seeds. I picked grape leaves from the front of the house for dolma. Her khuzi is my favorite Middle Eastern dish. It is a stuffed lamb cooked with saffron rice, slivered almonds, and raisins, similar to a stuffed turkey at Thanksgiving in the U.S. but with lamb. The rice stuffing rivals any turkey stuffing. When guests came over to visit Bibi, I served them tea and sweets. She enjoyed showing me off as her granddaughter. I loved serving her, helping in any way I could. It gave her such pleasure to have me there. Her presence was always a comfort to me.

One day, I wanted a glass of wine. I put on my *abaya*, a black veil covering me from head to toe, to walk over to the department store in our New Baghdad district. By then, my Arabic was fluent. Walking in, I looked around to make sure the coast was clear before I headed to the wine section. To my delight, the store had crystal wine glasses from Czechoslovakia and wine from France. The woman at the counter asked me if I was Kurdish because of my light eyes and skin tone. I said I was, eagerly looking over her shoulder to evaluate their wine selection. I asked her for a bottle of Beaujolais and four crystal wine glasses in a box. "Is this for your husband?" the store clerk asked. "Yes," I replied. I walked home with the package under my *abaya*. My left hand held the veil shut while my right hand was tightly positioned underneath to cover my purchase, in case I ran into family members.

When I arrived home, I quietly entered through the front door, concerned that my grandmother would greet me. Usually, I hung my veil on a hook next to my grandmother's other veils to the left side of the foyer entrance. This time, I kept it on and walked gently as quickly as possible without bringing much attention to myself, hoping no one would see me.

"Nadia." "Yes, Bibi?" I answered from a distance. "Come talk to me," she said from the kitchen.

"Let me just drop a few things off in my room," I replied. I went downstairs after securing my prohibited purchase in my room. Bibi shared her day with me. I discussed everything with her except my shopping spree at the department store. Later that evening, I told Bibi I needed to go upstairs to study. She excused me. Walking into my bedroom, locking the door, I retrieved the hidden bottle of wine only to realize I did not have a wine opener. I found a nail, and with my wooden Dr. Scholl's shoe I hammered the nail into the cork, then pulled it out. Pouring the wine into the beautiful crystal glass pleased me, in part, for claiming my underage Western heritage. My uncle's maid stopped by. I invited her in. Poor thing, she got drunk.

My uncle was walking around the perimeter of the house, calling her from the outside. She was giggling when responding, "I will be right down, Uncle." My family did not like that I was friends with a maid, someone deemed beneath me. You can have a warm relationship with the pretense of a family feeling. But when it came to social situations, the maid's station was never elevated to be equal. My uncle did drink; I am sure he could smell the alcohol on his maid's breath. She never stopped by again after that evening. I hid the unfinished bottle of wine behind the armoire. It wasn't until I left the country that I realized that someone would figure out who left the half-full bottle of wine.

The year was coming to an end. Speaking three languages at times confused me. Upon waking up in the dark, I had to get my bearings to figure out which country I lived in. Ten and a half months in Baghdad was all I could take. My uncle, who lived on the compound in our old home, wanted me to stay to finish my college degree in Baghdad. He tried bribing me into staying. One balmy summer evening, we sat outside on a swing. "Nadia, if you stay, finish your college degree here, we will go to Saudi Arabia to buy you whatever car you want. You can go to Europe twice a year to buy your clothes, and visit the U.S. once a year." I thanked him for his generosity, delicately declining the offer, to his disappointment.

I went to my other cousins' home to say goodbye. My aunt invited me to live with her to finish college with her daughters, my favorite cousins. I respectfully declined her offer as well.

My father was the only person who got it. "Nadia, you are American. You don't belong here in Baghdad. Go back to America," he said.

During my stay in Baghdad, I had eleven marriage proposals in ten and a half months. My time there was spent with family or in school. On a few occasions, I attended the club with my family; prospective husbands must have inquired about me after seeing me on those few outings. My uncle wanted me to consider some of the proposals.

Bibi had a stroke, a complication of her diabetes a few months before I left Baghdad. She was in a coma at the hospital. Her attending physician was from the Al-Samarrie tribe. He was 30 years old. Sitting in the hospital room holding my grandmother's hand, Ahmed, the doctor, told me he had a son he wanted me to marry. I told him I was not interested in getting married. Bibi's hospital stay was prolonged. Every day, sitting in her room after school, Ahmed came in to chat. The truth be told, he had no son, nor was he married. Eventually, he asked me to marry him. Bibi, whom I thought was in a coma, suddenly gained awareness of her surroundings, piping up, "That would be nice."

The doctor's overtures got more aggressive over time. He was the physician for the Prime Minister of Iraq - *Ahmed Hassan al-Bakr*. One day, he threatened me by saying, "I will turn you in as an American spy if you do not marry me." Fearing his threat, I told him I would give him an answer on a specific date. My uncle later asked me about marrying him. "Uncle," I said in Arabic, "Ahmed is 30. I am 19. I want someone my age who can dance with me." He laughed. What Ahmed did not know was that I had already booked a flight to Paris and planned on going to Munich to meet Margit. The date I told him I would give him an answer was three days past my departure.

I left Baghdad with mixed feelings. As much as I was ready to go, I knew this probably would be the last time I would see my beloved Bibi. As a child and teenager, I have had the same reoccurring dream with my grandmother. We are in a pyramid in Egypt, both standing at the end of a rectangular wooden table. She has a gift she wants to give me. It is in a wooden box. She reaches to open the box; then I wake up. This dream has not returned for quite a while now, but she was the most significant elder in my life.

My father took me to the airport. We hugged and kissed while saying our goodbyes. He watched me walk away and hand my passport to the guard. The security guard looked through my passport then said, "You cannot leave." I asked him why, fearing Ahmed's possible intervention. "Because your passport was not stamped when you entered the country. We need to know how you entered Iraq. If I let you pass, they can hang me."

My father watched from a distance as I returned to him. He seemed unfazed. "Don't worry. I will take care of it for you tomorrow." Tomorrow took two extra days. I was beginning to feel anxious about Ahmed and wanted to leave the country before I had to answer his marriage proposal. As a nineteen-year-old, surrounded by family who loved me, it did not occur to me to share Ahmed's threat with them because I wasn't sure who wanted me to marry him.

On the second departure date, I boarded the plane to leave Baghdad. We landed in Lebanon. I watched a Jeep with four armed men approach the plane. Fearing Ahmed's reach in imprisoning me, I sat in the airplane, taking shallow breaths, wondering if I would be apprehended. To my relief, some passengers disembarked. It was wasn't until the plane took off crossing the European border that I felt relief.

My mother wired me money to stay in Paris. Margit was to be home in one week. I stayed at a monastery within walking distance from Notre Dame. It had segregated accommodations for men and women. There was a youth group from Spain staying in Paris for an academic language experience. In the morning, the monastery served tea in what I call extra-large Alice in Wonderland cups. We had fresh baguettes with jam and fruit. I took in the sites, overall enjoying myself except for one day. A man kept following me everywhere I went. In frustration, I asked him to stop following me. He ignored my request, and kept stalking me until I stood in a four-way intersection screaming "police" as loud as possible. He quickly disappeared.

I went back to Munich after Margit came home. We decided to get jobs downtown. Margit found employment at a bakery. I got a job in an Italian restaurant that, at first, did not have an opening. Nor did I have legal documentation allowing me to work. I went in twice, asking to work for them. The owners said they could not hire me. I liked the restaurant so much; I offered to volunteer there just to practice my German. The owners, whom I loved, said they were Italian and French. I told them I did not care.

The place was Rodella's, an elegant restaurant near the opera house where well-heeled professionals came in to dine. I worked the bar serving beer, wine, and *aperitifs,* and made espresso drinks. My shift started with trimming and arranging flowers for the vases to be placed on the white tablecloths.

When the restaurant owners sat to eat, they insisted I sit with them. They drove me home in their Mercedes in the evenings with the sunroof open while we all sang Dean Martin's "Volarie." Learning of Dean Martin in Iran in the 1960s from his movies came in handy in Munich in the 1970s.

One weekend, Margit and I wanted to take a road trip. Her mother said we could go to Austria using her car. After we started our drive, we spontaneously decided to go to Northern Italy. The first border we went to did not allow us to enter the country. We could not enter Italy because the car we were driving was not registered in one of our names. We decided to drive through the Alps to Lake Como, entering Italy at a different border in the mountains. The Italian guards on duty there were drunk. They allowed us through the checkpoint without requesting the car's registration.

Northern Italy had many blond, blue-eyed Italians. At first, I was surprised. But then I realized the population is greatly influenced by the neighboring Germanic countries, where people are fair-skinned.

I can't remember where we stayed. But we had lots of fun. We played billiards, walked around, ate gelato, and rented a boat to picnic in with cheese and crackers. It was a beautiful June day when we went out on the lake, with our feet dangling over in the opposite direction, reading our Vogue magazines in English and German. Margit, a tall, beautiful, slender blonde, got a lot of attention from the Italian men. We learned to say *arrivederci* when we wanted them to leave us alone.

Another perfect summer with Margit came to an end. I did not realize that Margit and I would not meet up again for thirty-eight years.

Katherine and I in high school

my good friends- from bottom left to right- Julie, me, Audrey, Emily and Sarah

Katherine seeing me off at the airport

Katherine and I on my way to my gate at SFO airport

Thanksgiving in Stockton with Jamal and Aunt Miriam

Graduation day from Berkeley High

University of Baghdad student identification card

college field trip to the Walls of Babylon

*presenting my professor at the University of Baghdad with a gift at the end
of the year*

**Author's note- I could not find the one picture I have of Bibi to
include in this book.**

FROM BAGHDAD TO BERKELEY

Chapter 5
Shifting Gears

After a one-year absence, I needed time to decompress after returning from Baghdad, adjusting to what was once my lifestyle. My ability to come and go without family members being concerned about my whereabouts was liberating. Living in Baghdad, I had to accommodate my family's concerns about my Western habits. All social interactions were carefully watched, with the fear that I might speak to a male and how that would be perceived. My father once told me that people were talking about my behavior at the University of Baghdad.

Admittedly, while starving for an intellectual conversation, I met a Nigerian man on campus on a few occasions during an outdoor event. We sat next to each other on the bleachers, ate our lunch, discussed world politics, religion, living in the Middle East, and cultural values. I was the only American in all of the universities. My fair complexion made me a target for idle gossip. Concerned about the innocent act of meeting an intellectual person to discuss topics beyond family or marriage, I knew my satiating encounter had to come to an end. I knew it could become a hornet's nest with fabricated stories about who I was, what I was doing, and what my real intentions were. Being an American from an Iraqi family, I had to manage my image. I grew up in Berkeley, where some of my best friends' parents were professors at the University; intellectual dinner discussions were part of our social bond. Gender never played a role in our thought process.

On my first morning back in Berkeley, I jumped on my bicycle to go to visit my best friend, Katherine, at her apartment near the Berkeley Campus. Janis Joplin's lyrics, "Freedom is just another word for nothin' left to lose," embodied my sentiment. I was free and had nothing to lose by cycling to my friend's home - free to be myself with no worries about how my actions would be perceived.

The next day, I rode my bicycle to the Berkeley Pier. Starting from Martin Luther King Street, I made a right on University Avenue following the road to the Bay. I crossed the Highway 80 overpass, pedaling fast. I was extremely happy for no apparent reason. It was inexplicable. Inside, I was screaming with joy in anticipation of reaching one of my coveted cocooning spots. Before attending the University in Baghdad, I never appreciated spontaneity. It was a given growing up in Berkeley, a luxury not afforded to me in Baghdad.

At the end of the pier, I parked my bicycle against the wall, climbed the wooden fence, and seated myself at the highest point to look over the Bay facing San Francisco.

A famous journalist in the Bay Area by the name of Herb Caen coined the phrase "Baghdad by the Bay." His interpretation of San Francisco is historical, reminiscent of a city built near the Tigris and Euphrates rivers that had a growing economy inviting foreign trade. Growing up in Baghdad as a child certainly felt more international. The external world was more accessible to us. Our social group reflected the political climate from that period.

My new appreciation for the simple things made life refreshing. Perched on the end of the horizontal wooden pier, the cool breeze, the saltwater, the boats, the birds, the fishermen, my independence felt fresh. The places I used to frequent now had a new allure.

It is interesting to have had such a tumultuous high school experience. Still, the year I came back from Baghdad, there was no question that I would finish my college degree.

Walking on campus my first week, a man of color looked at me, turned to his friend, and said, "Look at her white legs." His tone implied there was something wrong with my skin tone. It made me laugh to hear him comment on the color of my complexion. I had just come back from Baghdad, where my light skin was considered an asset.

I was happy to get a job selling speed-reading courses just before school started. My boss was in his forties. He gave me a lot of latitude on how to approach my sales quotas. As a prerequisite, completing the speed-reading course required me to be more knowledgeable when discussing the program with prospective students. I enjoyed my work. Setting up my little table at colleges, in bookstores, speaking to other students with different academic goals, was fascinating.

After being trained and meeting my sales quotas, my boss started calling me in the evenings frequently under the guise of seeing how my workday went. It began to make me feel uncomfortable. There was no way out of the nightly conversations that were not on point regarding my work. My dinners would burn; the phone was far from the stove, and running over to turn off the stovetop burner was impossible. At nineteen, I sensed that my boss's phone calls were inappropriate. There was no way to confront him. Four months into the job, I quit in search of new employment.

I looked for a new job that would accommodate my school schedule. I was happy to get a job quickly at Giant Hamburgers. They offered me four shifts working 32 hours a week, morning and graveyard hours, with two 8 am to 4 pm shifts, and two 7 pm to 3 am shifts. In the mornings, I cooked breakfast for customers. In the afternoons and evenings, people ordered hamburgers and fries. I worked at both of their locations. At the Southside location near Telegraph, it was more dangerous to leave work at three in the morning. Not because of the homeless community on the street or People's Park; it was the drunken fraternity boys who were a threat.

After working at the Southside location, I became friends with a homeless man. He was a Vietnam vet, six-feet-two-inches tall with long, wavy brown hair. He wore green military fatigues with black military boots. He looked like he hadn't shaved in months. He always kept me company at Giant Hamburgers, regardless of my Northside or Southside location.

Every shift, he came in to sit at the end of the counter, quietly staring into his coffee cup for hours. I never feared him. Having him keep me company at work gave me great comfort. He usually stayed with me for my entire eight-hour schedule. We had an unspoken agreement. I knew he deterred lingering men waiting for me to get off work from harassing me. His size and expressionless face made him look unpredictable, intimidating the well-heeled younger men. He, on the other hand, needed shelter and was always welcome to stay when I was working. I passed no judgment on him. He was a man who served his country and was discarded by the government when it came to his mental health needs.

On the slow, quiet nights, I would hand him quarters throughout the early mornings over the counter for the jukebox. He would walk over and put a quarter in to play my favorite song, Leonard Skynyrd's "Free Bird." One day as I was ending my shift at three in the morning, a young fraternity man stalked me. He waited for me to get off work until he could approach me. When I finished my shift, I noticed him as I put on my helmet, ready to start my moped. Concerned for my safety, I turned the engine off and looked for my homeless veteran friend. He looked up from the sidewalk and watched me as I came and sat next to him. This made the stalker give up and disappear. I then jumped on my moped, quickly turned on the engine, and drove off as fast as it would go. I looked nervously and frequently in my mirrors to ensure that no one followed me in a car.

Later that year, I moved into an apartment with male roommates. One roommate, Tim, was a deckhand on a sport-fishing boat at the Berkeley Pier. He was a hardworking eighteen-year-old who woke up every day at 4 am. The walls between our bedrooms were thin. I knew what time it was in the morning by the loud weather report on his radio. It was the first thing he listened to before getting ready for work. If the weather was terrible for sport fishing, he needed to call the boat captain, who determined if they were going out that day to the Farallon Islands to fish.

I went out with him one morning for the experience. It was cold. The sky was grey, the water a bit choppy with deep swells rocking the boat as we headed toward the Golden Gate Bridge. While standing on the starboard deck, my gaze caught a massive movement. Something started to surface. The size scared me. Our boat was minuscule compared to whatever was about to rise. It was a metal object painted black. The moving body of water indicated it was going to be much larger than what was visible to the naked eye. Suddenly, a Navy submarine surfaced in the San Francisco Bay. The hatch opened. One person climbed up the ladder, and stood there with binoculars looking around from left to right. After a few minutes, he shut the hatch and the submarine descended underwater. This experience deterred me from ever swimming in the Bay. The unknown objects cruising below the waterway redefined my comfort exponentially.

Later, Tim took me out with another friend of his commercial fishing in the Bay. We found a school of fish using a detector on the boat. The two men had fishing poles with eight hooks; mine had four. Our fishing poles started to pull our wrists. We all had multiple fish on our lines. Commercial fishing with no bait falsely appeared to be prosperous. All we had to do was cast a line for fish to bite. Tim showed us how to unhook our catch. The fish kept flipping their bodies when we kneeled on one leg to remove the hook from their mouth gently. We placed them in a U-shaped water aquarium.

In the back of the boat, we were keeping the fish fresh. We caught rock cod for hours until the aquarium was full, heading back to Pier 39 after dark. The small boat did not have radar. The fog moved in. The return trip was dangerous. A sudden, large vessel could surprise us by running into our little boat. We stayed quiet, motionless, making our way back to the pier, listening for ships approaching us. Thankfully, we made it back safely. My friend took all but a few of the fish we caught to sell at one of the pier's restaurants.

Tim introduced me to his friends. A group of us used to hang out together after work. Several of my friends had motorcycles. I rode a moped for years. The limiting factor of my transportation was that I could not ride on the freeway. Riding on the back of my friend's beautiful red 750 Suzuki influenced me to upgrade to a faster bike.

One night, my friend Antony and I were on our way to Brennan's in Berkeley for an Irish coffee. It was a beautiful night. I listened to John Lennon's song "Imagine" on my headset, sitting on the back of his bike holding a CD player. The fresh air from the Bay brushed against me.

Antony's beautiful motorcycle felt like the Porsche of bikes. It influenced my decision to get a road motorcycle. I asked him if he could help me buy one and teach me how to ride it. He agreed to find me a bike that was within my budget.

A month later, a reddish-orange Kawasaki 400 came up for sale. We took his bike to go and look at it. I had the cash on hand if my friend deemed it was a good purchase. We rode tandem on Highway 13 to look at my new prospective motorcycle in Montclair. Our plan was not well thought out. The bike was at a resident's home on top of a steep hill. After my friend checked out the bike for me, deeming it a good purchase, he had to ride it down the steep driveway. I waited next to his motorcycle, watching him make his way down. My lesson on how to drive a bike was short. Antony showed me how to change gears with my hand when moving the clutch with my foot. We took off on a flat area to practice. I felt powerful riding a motorcycle for the first time.

Antony kept his eye on me through his side mirrors. I felt a bit nervous watching the direction he was riding in, unsure if we were going to take the backroads to Berkeley, when it suddenly dawned on me that he was taking the highway back home. His confidence in me dissolved my fear of not being qualified to drive the most direct route home.

Decades later, married with children, I reminded my friend of the short motorcycle lesson, followed by the entrance onto the freeway. He couldn't believe it. "That was so irresponsible of me," he said.

I loved having a motorcycle. Gas and insurance didn't cost much. It also allowed me to travel long distances. On Christmas Day, Antony and I drove to Stinson Beach from Berkeley. It was a warm day, uncharacteristic of the typical winter weather. The winding West Marin country roads are fun to ride on. I leaned far down into my turns, experimenting with my control until I found the perfect angel between my bike and the pavement. Stinson Beach was quiet. The early morning offered the pretense of a private beach with a light, calm wind. We walked on the sand and sat near a rock, emoting about the relationships in our lives.

This man was a good friend of mine for a long time. I introduced him to his wife. Knowing that they both had a crush on each other, I enjoyed bringing them together. They have been blessed with a long, happy marriage.

Once I became a seasoned rider, I gave people rides on my motorcycle. One year, a childhood friend from Baghdad came to visit. I picked her up in San Francisco from Berkeley. We got dressed up to go clubbing in the city. After dropping her off for the evening, I took the Bay Bridge back to the East Bay. I entered the bridge from downtown San Francisco. No one was on the road. I had never had an opportunity to see how fast my motorcycle could go. I decided to test my curiosity. I looked around to make sure no other cars were on the bridge. I tucked my head down and turned my wrist, accelerating full throttle to see how fast my motorcycle could go. To this day, I can feel the rush as I slowly increased my speed, ensuring I could maintain control while accelerating, going faster and faster. I passed Angel Island, making my way to Oakland when I heard a voice on a microphone say, "Would you please pull over."

I looked in my side mirror—a California Highway Patrol Vehicle with red sirens was behind me. My first thought was that they must have been pulling someone else over, until I realized it was me they were seeking to stop. They pulled over behind me. I brought my motorcycle to a halt, took my helmet off, and watched the California Highway Patrolman in my side mirror as he approached me from the back of my motorcycle.

I had curly thick hair past my shoulders, wore a white cashmere sweater, 501 jeans with a knee-high brown tweed coat, and heels. I knew I could be in big trouble– not only for speeding. I had a motorcycle permit that did not allow me to drive at night or on freeways. Furthermore, I had not registered the bike in my name, plus I had one drink.

"Good morning," I said to the CHP as he walked towards me.

"Do you know how fast you were driving?" he asked.

"No, officer," I responded.

"We clocked you at 100 miles per hour in a 55 mile per hour speed zone. Can I see your license and motorcycle registration?" he asked.

His partner sat on the passenger side with his door wide open watching from a distance. The CHP officer who took my documents walked back to his partner. I heard him say, "What are we going to do with her, Bob?" He checked my name through his database; everything came up clean. Now it was a matter of which violations he was going to cite me for. Coming back, he said, "I am not giving you a ticket for going 100 miles an hour in a 55-mile zone, not having your motorcycle registered, or for driving on the freeway after dark with a permit." He gave me a thirty-five-dollar speeding ticket and said, "Next time, don't drive so fast."

There was no question in my mind that, had I been a young male, they *might* have hauled me into jail. I believe I was an anomaly to them at that time. My audacity to go full throttle on the freeway intrigued them. The ticket was a small slap on my wrist. They followed me on the highway before I exited in Oakland, taking the back streets to my Berkeley home.

That same day, late in the afternoon, I raced my friend David on the streets in Oakland below the freeway. The absence of a muffler on his Honda 550 brought attention to our race. He passed the policemen while I was pulled over for the second time in one day. This ticket was not as forgiving as my last one. In both instances, my speed was almost double the posted speed rate. Knowing that if I got a third violation I could face a license suspension, I signed up for traffic school. The hefty citation turned out to be the best thing for me. The disturbing educational videos, especially motorcycle accidents, changed the way I drove on the road.

One thing about riding a bike - you generally are invisible to cars. Sitting at any stoplight, I never accelerated unless the vehicles were at a complete stop. Oil from leaky cars could cause me to fishtail when pulling out of a tollbooth. During wintery, rainy days, drivers came to a sudden halt, causing me to drive on the road dividers to prevent an accident. After two winters, I decided to sell my motorcycle to get a car. But I still wanted another bike, something that could go faster. I went to an establishment that sold racing bikes, owned by a bunch of young men who were determined to scare me away from riding. They viewed it as a man's sport. One guy gave me a ride on a racing bike that frightened me. Every time he changed gears, the bike would rise off the asphalt even though we were both on it. His efforts to deter me from owning another motorcycle worked. Subsequently, I never rode a bike again.

After leaving Giant Hamburgers and getting a job at a cafe, I saw my Vietnam vet friend only when I was on Telegraph Street. We acknowledged each other with a smile and a head nod to say, "Hey, I see you, and I still have your back." One day he disappeared forever.

The cafe was at the end of College Street in Berkeley, bordering the city of Oakland. Two good friends were inspired to open a breakfast and lunch establishment. One of them previously worked for a lawyer who represented one of the Black Panther Party founders, Huey Newton. After his release from jail, Huey frequented the cafe. I will never forget the first day I waited on him. Incognizant of his historical role in the Black Panther movement, I approached him as I did all customers, in a chirpy voice. "Good afternoon, what can I get for you?" I asked. He deliberately took his time, paused, looked into my eyes, and said in a disturbing voice, "What are you so happy about? Don't ever look at me that way again."

When he spoke to me for the first time, I looked into his eyes, sensing a dark and tortured soul. Looking away from him, I said, "OK, do you know what you would like to eat?" He placed his order. My boss saw him after I took his order. They were excited to greet each other. Huey had a softer disposition with him.

Before Huey's release from jail, my boss was one of my roommates. Sometimes, Huey called us on our one landline at 2 am, and I usually answered. He was gruff, demanding to speak to my roommate. Back in the early 1980s, bugging private citizens was not that advanced. I could always hear a click when Huey called my home. He set the tone for my interaction with him. I always kept it short, absent of small talk.

His death was upsetting to me. Even though my personal experience with him felt unsafe at times, I could feel his tortured soul post-incarceration, and felt compassion for a man who struggled. His desperate solution of bearing arms during a socially and politically volatile time in history forever changed his life. The passionate man archived in the video footage was somewhat vacant, ready to defend himself at the drop of a hat. Prison dampened his spirit.

Halloween - wearing my nightgown and clogs to the cafe on my orange Kawasaki 400

salmon fishing with Timmy at the Farallon Islands

catching my first salmon - sport fishing on Timmy's boat

Chapter 6
Going Down Under

After four years of service with the U.S. Navy, my brother Jamal knew Western Australia was still an undiscovered territory. He felt he would have more professional opportunities to choose from because he did not plan on going back to school to pursue a college degree. In search of a high-paying job to support his new family, he left the Bay Area, relocating to Perth to purchase a home. His work took him further north in the bush. He came home periodically to visit his family.

My mother and I missed him dearly. She decided to take a trip to Australia, offering to pay for all my expenses if I would join her. I quit my job waiting tables at the cafe to board a plane days after her departure. I sat next to a Jewish man who said he was the founder of Caterpillar machinery. We spent the long twenty-something hour flight discussing the Middle East with the challenges that face the Arabs and Israelis.

By the time we arrived in Sydney, we had developed a kinship for one another, exchanged mailing addresses to stay in touch. I had a long layover in Sydney. I decided to take a bus into the downtown area to explore the famous Sydney Opera House, overlooking the Harbor Bridge with the charming neighboring districts. What surprised me the most about my bus ride into town was the architecture. The metalwork on some of the homes' balconies reminded me of the French district in New Orleans. It was a beautiful design of ironwork, like the template I had to create for my *Show Boat* musical production when I was seventeen.

The Sydney Opera House was spectacular. I toured the empty building early in the morning, peeking into temporarily closed rooms. Most of the opera houses I have attended are in historic architectural buildings. The Sydney Opera House is novel — a bold, iconic modern design that is unforgettable.

After spending the day in Sydney, I boarded a plane to Perth. The flight lasted five hours. Jamal greeted me at the airport. Once he spotted me disembarking, he walked towards me, giving me a warm smile that could melt snowcaps. Elated to see him again, we hugged, happy to have an opportunity to be back in each other's company. What made it more meaningful was knowing my visit would be limited in time. My mother and I stayed with him in the first home he bought at twenty-three. My second nephew was born there shortly before my arrival.

Perth in 1982 was extremely provincial. Jamal's home was far from the city. He lived in a new development in the suburbs, with empty lots that were yet to be built on. With no nightlife to speak of, the bars were the few social places where people could meet. American sailors frequented the bars once their ship docked. They have a custom there called "Dial a Sailor," a tradition where local Aussies invite American sailors to come to their home for dinner after they dock. It's a welcoming hospitality gesture.

Arriving sailors clean their ships before nearing the dock to showcase their seaworthy carrier. The sailors disembark looking dapper in their U.S. Navy uniforms, enthusiastic about exploring Perth. Australian women go to the pier to meet and greet the sailors to invite them to their homes for dinner. My brother met his wife through this welcoming tradition.

I went into a pub to rest after sightseeing and ordered a beer to relax before I took the train back home. An American sailor approached me to chat. I encouraged him to pursue Aussie women if he wanted to learn more about Australia. Further sharing what my sixteen-year-old sister-in-law's brother taught me, Aussie men preferred their cars, beer, then women, in that order. The Australian women preferred American men because they preferred their women, cars, and then beer.

One day, I asked my brother if I could take his car out for a drive to see the countryside. I was a bit nervous as he lived in a rural area at the time. Knowing which side of the road to drive on was perplexing. Road-kill kangaroos lay dead on the highway. When I was driving down a two-lane street, I saw a car approach me. I realized I was on the wrong side of the lane, quickly pulled over, and came to a sudden stop. My two-year-old godson Caesar was in his car seat. I was stressed, so I decided to sit in the car for a few minutes. I asked God to keep my godson and myself safe when driving on the opposite side of the street. After the car passed, I got back on the road. Eventually, I became comfortable driving in Australia. Once I mastered driving on the left side of the street, there was not much to see locally.

One of my favorite places we frequented was Freemantle. The city, established in 1829, is one of the Swan River Colonies. Later Freemantle received world recognition for becoming a famous stop in the World Cup sailing race. My mother, brother, and I went there for lunch and a walk. One sizeable wooden building we entered looked like an old hangar for boats, redesigned to house several businesses. Freemantle in the early 1980s was quaint, rustic, still undiscovered.

Jamal took us to the brewery in Perth to see how they made beer. We learned that all employees received a case of beer a day. Some workers claimed their beer early in the morning, drinking a few of them during their lunch break. Later the company changed its corporate policy as to when the employees could have the case of alcohol: after work was the newly designated pickup time.

We frequented a teashop in downtown Perth across the street from the post office to have tea and crumpets. Later, we went wine tasting in Swan Valley. I purchased several nice bottles of wine to bring home, which unfortunately broke in my luggage. Custom officers in Los Angeles, California, were just as surprised as I was to see my clothes marinated in red and white wine when I opened my luggage for inspection.

As much as I loved my brother, I was a bit bored in Perth after one month. At twenty-four years old, my brother was a married man with two children, working hard to support his family. I wanted to explore, travel farther. Given his family obligations, he did what he could to entertain us. After my godson's baptism at the church, I decided to go to Tahiti on my way back home. It was a destination that was a stopover on my round-trip ticket through Qantas Air. My funds were limited. I did not want to ask my mother for money. As an independent twenty-three-year-old, I was too proud to ask for help. I accepted her assistance when I needed it. But overall, I declined her aid.

I arrived in Tahiti, checking into a small hotel. It was more like a *pensione*, a boarding house with limited rooms in a charming location within walking distance to the downtown marina. Having come from a different time zone, I woke up late that morning. My summer in Australia was cold. Anxious to enjoy warm weather and white sand beaches, I strolled from my accommodations to downtown Papeete. I felt joyful, happy to be in the distant French South Seas, walking with a skip in my step. I softly gazed at the Bay, the shops, the docked boats at the pier, when my eyes suddenly focused on a "help wanted" sign. The captain of a sailing boat had posted a flyer, looking for a crewmember to sail to Hawaii. The sense of adventure inspired me to walk over to speak with the captain. I made my way to the dock, walked up the slip, and stood in front of the boat, my commitment suddenly wavering. I felt the need to deliberate more, trusting my hesitation. It felt like a once-in-a-lifetime opportunity. My imagination took me to open waters, curious if I would see whales or dolphins, or if a great white shark could attack the small sailboat. I asked myself if I could trust an unknown captain to have the skill set to navigate treacherous weather conditions.

I decided to take my time weighing in the pros and cons. I was in Tahiti for one week and did not feel an urgency in deciding to crew. Every time I made my way down to the sailboat, I hesitated. My biggest concern was being a single woman boarding a boat where my family would have no idea where I was. If anything happened to me, I could be an unsolved mystery. Dan, a friend of mine in high school, saved money by bagging groceries to travel around the world. The last place he was spotted was taking a boat to a remote area in India. As a single woman who went to Europe by herself, I already had a flavor of the ugly things men can try to do to a woman. As much as the sea beckoned me, I realized I could be raped, dumped in the ocean without a sign of my whereabouts—no smartphone or GPS to identify my last location.

My time in Europe visiting museums turned me into an art aficionado. While in Tahiti, I learned of Gauguin's history. Tahiti was where he created some of his unforgettable collection. Gauguin's paintings tell the story of how the local people lived. He illustrated the Tahitian lifestyle through his paintings, introducing the world to an unknown culture. His artwork traveled back to Paris for people from all around the world to view.

The Gauguin museum was in the countryside, a good hike from the downtown area. The only bus I could take dropped me off in a seemingly rural setting. I hitched a ride in a white truck, sitting in the back of the bed with a group of Tahitians who were to be dropped off in a farming district. My last few miles required a foot trek. Walking on the right side of the road, I could see a man in the fields from a distance, on the road's left side. He stopped what he was doing, stared at me, and started to walk in my direction. Feeling anxious, alone in an uninhabited rural area, I stuck my thumb out, hoping to catch a ride. To my relief, a car stopped; two American women were heading to the Gauguin Museum.

We approached what looked like a Japanese-style building that housed the Museum. When the women parked the car, I got out and thanked them for the ride. Just standing at the entrance made the trip worth it. I was excited to see Gauguin's larger-than-life masterpiece collection from the late 1800s. I paid my entrance fee, received a brochure, and walked through a small, modest building to look for large pieces of Gauguin's art. To my great disappointment, the Museum did not have one original Gauguin painting on display. Instead, they had card-sized images of his work with a notation of where the art is displayed—most of them were in the United States.

Leaving the Museum after a short stay, I felt uncomfortable asking the same women who picked me up to give me a ride back to Papeete. This time, I stood outside of the Museum, hitchhiking in a more populated area where people could see who was picking me up.

A small white pickup truck, filled with loud, live chickens in cages stacked to the top of the back window, stopped. The driver's entire body was tattooed. He rolled down his window to inform me of his destination. I had to assess the level of danger this ride might put me in, speaking English with sign language. The driver spoke some English, although his presentation made him questionable. I went with my gut feeling; I would be safe riding along with him to my next destination.

When we got closer to my destination, he taught me how to ask for directions in French. I wrote it down phonetically, knowing that I might not remember the exact words. He took me as far as he could go, instructing me on how to get back to town and away from my rural surroundings.

After he dropped me off, I hitchhiked again. A sweet family with two young children picked me up. They wanted to take me to see the

Cascades of Faarumai, a beautiful waterfall. Meeting these people helped me understand why Gauguin was so enamored with the Tahitian hospitality. The family later drove me to the main road after they invited me to come to their home for lunch.

I hitched one last time; a man in an open Jeep picked me up. He was handsome, well-groomed, and wanted me to know that he was affluent. He invited me to join him on his helicopter to stay at his home on the island of Bora Bora. I politely declined and told him that I had dinner plans with my family, whom I was meeting up with later. He dropped me off at the marina downtown. Walking back to my hotel, I looked for the "Crew Wanted" sign, curious to know if they filled their position. In some ways, I felt tormented. I wanted to jump on the boat to sail the high seas, but because I could not guarantee my safety, it was best to leave it as a fantasy.

The next day I decided to go to the island of Moorea. Approaching the boats at the port, I saw a group of loud Americans getting ready for a week at Club Med. I did not want to be associated with them. Instead of taking the cruise liner they boarded, I decided to board a cargo ship. The vessel, docked next to the luxury cruise, carried goods to the next island. There was one other passenger outside of the crew and me. Once the cargo ship departed, the view of the South Pacific Ocean in French Polynesia was breathtaking. I remember standing in the middle of the top deck, thinking I used to believe Hawaii was heaven; the Hawaiian waters were pale compared to this part of the world. A crewmember started to play the ukulele. I took a deep breath encapsulating the moment of still water in a gorgeous open ocean. A Polynesian man serenaded us by singing an enchanting, peaceful, calming song as the ship waded through the South Pacific Ocean to the next island.

The cruise liner reached the Moorea port before the cargo ship. The loud, obnoxious sounds of the Americans deterred me from hitchhiking.

While on foot, they passed me. Their drivers picked them up in black Jeeps. The caravan of cars brushed against the green island foliage driving away from the dock. The Americans' voices echoed with excitement. I could still hear them from a distance.

Walking with no map in hand, miles away from the port, I found an uninhabited white sand beach. I lay my belongings down, and walked into the warm ocean water. I swam, floated on my back, and looked up at the blue sky. I was in awe of this magnificent, isolated beach that was all mine. Spending hours going in and out of the water, napping on the white sand, I then walked back to the port to catch the cargo boat back to Papeete.

On my last day, when it was time to leave Tahiti, a 1960s 404 Peugeot taxied me back to the airport. It all seemed so divine. I loved that make and model of car. It was the first car I ever purchased for myself, a white 1962 404 Peugeot with five gears on a column and a sunroof. My taxi felt like a positive omen. A sign that I would be home soon, safe, in my familiar surroundings.

Jamal in the Navy

Jamal and Caesar pick me up at the Perth airport

my adorable godson Caesar

FROM BAGHDAD TO BERKELEY

Chapter 7
Jack London Square

Finding work after my Tahiti trip was more difficult than I imagined. It took me four months to find a job. My savings account was dwindling. Humbled by having no paycheck in sight, a friend lent me rent money just before I started working as a banquet waitress at Jack London Square.

Being a banquet waitress near the waterfront in Oakland was different from Berkeley. Unlike the part-time students working their way through college, the employees were long-term restaurant professionals accustomed to working on a sophisticated computer system. There was a corporate culture that was unfamiliar to me. Thursday nights offered a lingerie-modeling event. Mostly men came in to view the bedroom attire. After the show, patrons could purchase the clothes. Doubting the legitimacy of the evening left me unsure, with mixed emotions. My station was in the back of the restaurant. The models were visible to me only when I crossed the floor to pick up drinks from the front bar.

The short-lived Oakland Invaders frequented the banquet rooms. The football team was replacing the Oakland Raiders during their brief departure to Southern California.

Famous players sat behind a long table in the front of the room. Local media dominated the space, hollering questions as camera flashed.

I met my next roommate there — a local woman who grew up in the Bay Area. We rented a beautiful apartment near Lake Merritt. We flipped a coin to see who would get the master bedroom with a walk-in closet and bathroom. It was my lucky day.

My roommate attended the university while I finished up my junior college requirements to transfer to a university. We got along well, considering I worked and lived with her. She was an incredibly talented artist who ended up dropping out of school. I suspect her drinking problem played a role in that decision. She was intelligent and levelheaded until she drank. Once she started drinking, her inhibitions disappeared. One night while out clubbing, she brought two men home. I was sound asleep in my room and didn't hear the party of three.

I woke up a bit later in the dark to a stranger in my room, caressing my face. I sat up, pushing myself away from the man and asked him to leave my room. Thankfully, he did. The next morning, after my roommate's guests left, I approached her about what happened. I was upset with her. She endangered my well-being. "What were you thinking?" I asked.

"I didn't know which man I wanted to be with, so I brought them both home," she said. "The second man left the room when he knew I didn't want to be with him." "What did you think he was going to do after he left your bedroom?" I asked. "I didn't think about it," she responded.

"Please never bring two men home at the same time unless you know what you are doing with them." She promised me it would never happen again. It never did.

The year went by quickly. I finished my university prerequisites to apply to Berkeley and San Francisco State University. Berkeley sent my application back, asking me to fill in which department I wanted to attend. I had already received an acceptance letter from San Francisco State University, so I decided to go there. I also wanted to have the experience of living in San Francisco instead of the East Bay.

My second roommate also worked with me. We shared a beautiful Victorian duplex in San Francisco with a gay man from work. It was in the Potrero Hill district on Philadelphia Street overlooking a breathtaking view of the South Bay. I moved there before starting at the University, still working in Oakland at Jack London Square. The restaurant owner, unbeknownst to me, was dating my San Francisco roommate.

One day, the restaurant owner made a pass at me in front of my two friends. I refused his overtures. He called my manager and had me fired under the grounds that I was insubordinate. My manager was a good friend of my San Francisco roommate. She gave me that look when she fired me —that there was nothing she could do, but she let me go.

Losing my job was untimely. I called my union representative to file a complaint about being unfairly fired. My rep did nothing. I continued to wait for a meeting with the restaurant management. I couldn't let it go. I thought about what a disgusting man the restaurant owner was, having made a pass at me, then punishing me financially because I would not return his flirtations. 'Hell No!" I thought. He is not going to get away with it. I decided to circumvent my local representative by calling the union headquarters in Sacramento. I asked to speak to the top union executive who oversaw the local representatives. The secretary asked me, "Who is calling?" "Nadia," I answered. The executive took my call immediately.

"Nadia, how are you?" he asked in a friendly voice.

"I am fine. Thank you," I responded. "I am calling about my case, the one where the restaurant owner fired me because I refused to be sexually harassed by him. He had management place a complaint in my file for being insubordinate and stealing a raw chicken breast."

"I am sorry," he responded. "I thought you were someone else. Nadia is not a common name."

"Yes, I know," I said, continuing. "I filed a complaint with my local representative. He has been ineffective in getting a meeting for me."

"I will see what I can do for you," he replied. I thanked him for his time. Two days later, my union representative called to let me know that he secured a meeting with the management. We met with them at the restaurant seated in a dining room, closed to the public. They offered me a small sum of money. My representative felt I should be pleased with the five hundred dollars. I accepted the settlement with mixed feelings, happy that the owner got slapped for his indiscretion while feeling disgruntled about the dollar amount.

When leaving my house in San Francisco in the morning for school, the landlady who lived in the top flat asked me when we were going to pay rent. "What do you mean?" I asked.

"You are six months behind on your rent," she said. Shocked, I explained that I paid my roommate, the man who had the lease in his name. I knew my male roommate had a drinking problem. Later I learned he also had a cocaine addiction. My rent money supplemented his substance abuse. It was a strange period in my life. My roommate's substance abuse was new to me, something I did not share with my Berkeley friends.

Anticipating an eviction, I started asking friends at the University if they knew of any rentals. At that time, a studio in San Francisco was six hundred dollars a month. My friend Kim asked me what my budget was. "Three hundred dollars," I answered. She told me it would be tough. A few days later, she told me she found a one-bedroom apartment for three hundred dollars, utilities included. If I wanted it, I needed to see it right away. I called my sister Mimi to join me in case I needed to negotiate the terms.

The apartment, formerly a garage converted into a living space, had one bedroom, a living room, office, a bar with highchairs for dining, a kitchen, bathroom, and a large back yard with a beautiful view of the city and freeway. It was on Monterey Boulevard in the Sunnyside district. I took the apartment and asked my new landlord if I could use my first month's rent to get new carpeting, paint, and linoleum floors in the kitchen and bathroom. She was pleased with my enthusiasm. I enjoyed updating my new apartment. My landlady, Hilda, and I grew to adore one another. She spoke English with a Spanish accent. We talked through a wall, downstairs in her foyer, which backed up to my office. Sometimes she would invite me upstairs to have tea with her. I can still hear her sweet voice, "Nadia, I am in my pa yam as (pajamas); let me change first and come up for tea." We had a loving relationship that continued to develop over six years.

My sister helped me get a job at a well-known Berkeley restaurant, 4th Street Bar & Grill before moving to my new residence. The new employment came with health insurance. It took me thirty minutes to drive from my San Francisco home to Berkeley. The freeway entrance was only a few blocks away on both sides of the Bay. I started as a bus person, working my way up to wait tables. It was an elegant restaurant that attracted celebrities and government officials. Chefs from other states took notes while dining. They expressed their pleasure for the food with sounds and facial expressions.

I waited on prominent businesspeople and celebrities. The only time I was left a lousy tip was from two famous actors. As a teenager, I loved their television show. But I was not fawning all over them at the restaurant because they were well-known performers. They kept dropping hints. I pretended to be obtuse. I served them like everyone else. They ordered their food; I served it on time, chatted with them a bit, and did not make a big deal about who they were. After they left, they wanted to insult my service by leaving me a penny. As if to say, "this is all you are worth." I couldn't believe what cheapskates they were with such fragile egos.

The restaurant also attracted many intellectuals, entrepreneurs, screenwriters, and people from recording studios. The wait staff was required to eat the food and try the wines before opening the doors to serve the public. We learned which wines paired with which entrée, making us better servers when customers asked for recommendations.

One day, at a staff meeting, we had a new employee join us. He was to wait on the best nights of the week. Unlike the rest of us, he was not required to climb the ranks by bussing tables before getting the coveted evening shifts. This announcement ruffled many of us. On my first day working with the new hire, I was filling butter in small, round, ceramic containers in the kitchen. Christian, the woman I was working with, looked through the round glass windows from the French swinging kitchen doors "He is cute," she said.

I walked away from my station, looked through the window for one second, and said: "He's OK."

The new employee introduced himself to me. He had just transferred to Berkeley to study mathematics. He was a gay man. We became good friends. We used to call each other to discuss how we felt about the people we were dating. Slowly, we both started canceling our dates, hanging out, and enjoying each other's company. Six months after going out to restaurants on our days off, jogging before a shift began at work, my new friend Scott made my bed for me as he usually did. I spent the night at his house once a week on his sofa bed in the living room. Since he was gay, I did not think much of it when he stayed in bed with me. I was straight — nothing was going to happen, in my mind. But it did. Everything changed after that for us.

Both the gay and straight communities were baffled by our romantic relationship. It threatened their definition of who they thought we were. A straight and gay person knew their social standing within the confines of their friendships. When this barrier is crossed, it confuses them with uncertainty. I think because it cast doubts on their roles, just like how I felt safe being myself with a gay man, knowing nothing would ever happen. After all, the line in the sand is defined by our sexual preferences. Life has a funny way of surprising us when we do the unthinkable, redefining who we will accept as our partner.

There was a more significant backlash from the gay community. Naively, I believed they would be happy for Scott. Instead, they felt abandoned when their good friend crossed over to be with a woman. It was incomprehensible, especially with how difficult it is to come out of the closet as a gay man. Then he chose a traditional relationship? I understand their perspective.

I shared my confusion about Scott with my Catholic Great Aunt Mary. When I started having feelings for my gay friend, in my mind, nothing would ever happen. It was even more confusing for me when my great aunt encouraged me to have a relationship with him. It wasn't until I was in my forties that I realized she encouraged the romance probably because she thought of it as faith healing. God brought me into his life to straighten him out. My siblings were not too keen about my relationship with a gay man. They were respectful with caution.

Scott, my new boyfriend, moved out of his Berkeley apartment to move in with me. He encouraged me to quit waiting tables during my last year of college. This way, he could support me in completing my university degree. As scary as it was, I trusted him with some trepidation. Never have I given up my source of income to be dependent on anyone. It was scary. But at the same time, it felt right. I finished college just before my twenty-eighth birthday from San Francisco State University with a Bachelor's in Science in International Business and Marketing.

After graduating from the university, Scott and I eloped on the Big Island of Hawaii at the Botanical Gardens. His cousin arranged the minister and traditional Hawaiian flowers one wears during a wedding ceremony. Unbeknownst to us, Scott's aunt and grandmother had purchased tickets to be there with his cousin, before we decided to elope.

They were the only attending family members at our wedding. We spent two weeks exploring the island, taking long horseback rides on ranches, and visiting black sand beaches up North.

After coming back from our honeymoon, I started looking for work. At first, I wanted to be a buyer for an upscale San Francisco store, I. Magnin. Meeting people in the retail industry was discouraging, causing me to look for work in a different sector—the financial market. I liked the stock market and felt it would be a fun job to have.

Scott stayed at the restaurant when I went out on job interviews. My first prospective employment was with Merrill Lynch in San Mateo. I was given a math and economics test. After passing both exams, I interviewed with the office manager. Sitting with him, I knew the interview was going well. He was going to hire me before I said, "There is one thing I need you to know."

"What is that?" he asked.

"I cannot make financial recommendations that are not in the client's best interest," I said.

The manager did not hesitate. He stood up, extended his hand to shake mine, and said, "Thank you for coming in."

My next interview was with Thomson McKinnon Securities, the largest privately-held securities firm on Wall Street. They were one hundred five years old. My conversations with management took thirteen hours in three different locations before they hired me. My boss knew how I felt about making financial recommendations that are not in the client's best interest, yet he added me to his sales team. I was happy to start working. It allowed my husband to quit his job while I supported him during his last year at the university.

After graduating from Berkeley with a degree in Mathematics, Scott accepted a job as an actuary with Wyatt, the second-largest cafeteria benefit plan in the United States. The job required a series of math exams. Most people do not pass them the first time around. Shortly after starting his work, Scott took his first test and passed with high marks. His success, unfortunately, created a toxic, jealous environment. Coworkers who failed the test on multiple occasions felt threatened by his success. They started making unsubstantiated, superficial complaints to his manager, which took time and effort to resolve.

At that juncture in our lives, we both started disliking our work cultures. I hated my job as a financial consultant. I loved stocks and investing, but the work environment was toxic.

We discussed leaving our jobs. Occasionally, we reminisced about the previous restaurant work that we enjoyed. The simplicity of wearing white t-shirts with a green and red pepper logo, a green apron, and a wine opener was all we needed. Now we wore grey suits and red ties, and carried briefcases. Working as white-collar professionals, we were exposed to mean-spirited, jealous colleagues that strategically worked with management on our demise.

Every morning driving downtown on the Sunnyside district's freeway, we could see the downtown San Francisco skyline, a view we once appreciated. When we started hating our jobs, the city skyline represented "The Temple of Doom." It became a place that made us unhappy.

My firm's corporate coach called me from New Jersey regularly. His job was to support me in building my client base—my book. He always started his calls with "are you naked?" before discussing my marketing efforts. One of the office managers was having an affair with his secretary, which was challenging to witness. I felt bad for his second wife. I had met her with their kids at an office picnic party. The woman who sat next to me had a heart attack. The company hired two sleazy, boiler room guys from an investment company that was closed and under investigation.

When I worked late to build my business, two associate brokers would call my extension after hours. They put our conversation on speaker, pretending to be significant investors to ridicule and mock me. I called them out on it and hung up. There was one man who always called me "Honey" with every encounter I had with him. I reminded him that my name is Nadia. He refused to call me by my first name.

One stockbroker was celebrated weekly in our sales meetings. His success was considered a goal we all needed to aspire to. When the Security Exchange Commission came in to handcuff him, management lowered their heads in disapproval, as if they had no idea what he was doing.

When friends and family asked me what it was like to be a stockbroker, I told them to watch the movie "Wall Street." It was such a relief to have a popular film illustrate the details of my work environment. It made me realize I was not crazy for feeling that something was very wrong in my work culture.

I started to hate my job and desperately wanted to create change. I knew if I stayed working there, it was just a matter of time before I had a health crisis. The problem I had with leaving is that it took a great deal of effort to get hired in the financial industry. It is a profession dominated by white men. My prospect of changing jobs scared me. I felt hopeless in creating the change I needed to find a better work environment.

One morning, Scott said, "Let's go to a Tony Robbins Fire Walk conference." In 1990 it was expensive. I was reluctant. But we both hated our jobs. I couldn't decide what to do.

Tony Robbins is a motivational speaker who teaches students "mind over matter," meaning your thoughts direct your actions. His approach was extremely novel; all you had to do was walk over hot coals. Yes, like the coals in your barbecue. It sounded ridiculous to me. But Scott reminded me how much we both hated our jobs; we had to keep moving forward until we found our way. He was right, and I knew it. I could pretend at work that everything was OK but not at home. There was a reason why many of my coworkers were having heart attacks.

A few days after the Fire Walk conversation, I told Scott I would participate in everything but the Fire Walk. Tony Robbins had already factored in people like me who wanted to watch from the sidelines. We arrived at the event, a three-day conference with thousands of excited people motivated about creating change in their lives. The Fire Walk is scheduled at the end of the evening on the first day. Tony explained that even if we did not want to walk over coals, we needed to stay in line until it was our turn. He said we could step out of the line once it is our turn. We left the conference hall late at night, winding our way outside onto a lawn with tiki lights illuminating the path. Tony instructed us to chant, "Cool mas, cool mas." Imagine thousands of people in rows chanting "Cool mas, cool mas," making their way down to the coals, excited about the experience. My reptile brain feared being involved in a cult when feeling vulnerable in life, just like the poor Moonie followers.

I broke my chant periodically, walking towards the hot coals, reminding Scott that I had no intention of walking on them. He was supportive in telling me to go ahead and step aside when my turn came up.

Standing in front of the hot coals, I decided to walk to the other side. I remember thinking, "Oh my God! I cannot believe I am doing this." The minute I stopped my chanting and thought about what I was doing, I could feel a burn on my left foot near the arch. In response to the burning sensation on my foot, I started chanting, "Cool mas, cool mas" again, walking ever so quickly over the coals to get to the other end. Completing the Fire Walk, I felt exhilarated. Still doubting myself, I could not believe I had walked on hot coals. It had to be a scam, I thought. I walked back to the coals just as someone finished their Fire Walk. I knelt, lowered my right hand as low as possible before feeling a temperature change in the coals to test if it was a lighting effect. This was no scam—they were hot. I quickly removed my hand to avoid being burned.

I learned a lot that weekend about my limiting thoughts and what I can and cannot do. Most notably, we create change in our lives for only two reasons: to feel better or to stop feeling bad. Another important concept that I learned is if I want to do something, like start a new business, don't reinvent the wheel. Study what successful people do and model them.

Scott and I walked away from the conference exhilarated. We decided to quit our jobs, go back to waiting tables, and start a new business.

working at 4ᵗʰ Street Bar & Grill in Berkeley

going to San Francisco State University from my new one bedroom apartment

Graduation from SFSU with a Bachelor of Science in International Business and Marketing

married at the Botanical Gardens in Hilo Hawaii

Botanical Gardens in Hilo Hawaii

horseback riding in Wailea Hawaii

Great Aunt Mary who encouraged me to be with Scott

Great Aunts- Sister Annetta, me, Mary, Virginia, mom and Cousin Diane

Financial Consultant for Thomson Mc Kinnon Securities

mom, Mimi and I upstairs at Chez Panisse Café in Berkeley

Chapter 8
Sugar Happy

Scott was diagnosed with Type 1 diabetes as a teenager. He made his self-care look easy. I assumed everyone was like him. He is bright, progressive, a visionary who is always ahead of the curve.

We deliberated over what type of business to start after our Fire Walk conference. We both have great memories of being on our family ranches and farms. I recommended we start a mail-order business so we could live anywhere. The medical industry at that time was a recession-proof industry. Our new goal was to live in the countryside, have a family, work from home, and have a farm and a horse.

We started a business we knew a lot about: diabetes and diabetes supplies. The company started from my college apartment in San Francisco. We named it Sugar Happy with a tag line "For Happy Blood Sugar Levels." Scott set up the back end of the business. I handled sales and marketing. We started with a one-page flyer that I distributed to clinics that saw patients with diabetes. We competed by offering reasonable prices, excellent service, and quick delivery—next day in most cases. The phone started ringing. "Sugar Happy Diabetes Supplies, how may I help you?" I asked.

It was exciting when we started getting customers without a storefront, just using UPS to send out medical supplies. Every day we received more phone calls. The challenge was getting the packages out before 3 pm, our UPS delivery deadline—that is if we wanted our customers to receive their medical supplies the next day.

We outgrew my college apartment in six months, forcing us to move to a lovely two-bedroom apartment near Sutro Park in the Outer

Richmond District. We had the top of a duplex that is known as a Doledger flat. Below us lived a tenant with mental health issues, making our two-year stay there extremely difficult. We moved the business again, this time to a storefront down the street to accommodate our growth.

On opening day, we invited the mayor of San Francisco, Frank Jordan, to cut the ribbon for our Grand Opening. He accepted our invitation. An enthusiastic crowd was waiting for the ribbon to be cut, ready to celebrate our opening with sugar-free snacks and view the store. We stocked books, travel cases, vitamins, supplements, blood glucose meters, syringes lancets, and strips.

Within one year of moving to our storefront, Scott encouraged me to start my own radio show. I have always been interested in women's issues. I started a program I named "A Women's Affair." Every week, my stomach would get upset just before I went live on the radio show. Scott was a great coach. "Just talk to them like you talk to everyone else, you're a natural," he said. I interviewed Nancy Pelosi, Barbara Boxer, women's organizations, and everything relevant and current to women's issues. It was fun.

One day, Scott received a call from someone in Guam who wanted him to speak at a diabetes conference. He kept putting the man off, hoping he would stop calling. Finally, Scott said, "I will consider it if my wife can come along. But I know my wife will not go unless the children go."

The man said, "We would love to host you all." Scott came into my office to tell me about his conversation with the man from Guam. "He wants me to speak at a conference; are you interested in going to Guam with the children?" "That could be fun," I said. We had a large staff running different departments who were able and willing to handle our absence.

After leaving San Francisco in 2002 for Guam, we had a layover in Japan for one night. Our host arranged for someone to pick us up at the airport and check us into our hotel. The taxicab driver told us, "We will be passing the American Embassy soon." Looking out the window, we passed by McDonald's. I asked him which building it was. "McDonald's is what we call the American Embassy." "That is terrible," I responded.

I have always loved Japan. My father was transferred to Tokyo in 1965 to stimulate trade between Iraq and Japan. Our first day there, after taking two taxis to our new home on Kami Migaro, my brother John's absence went unnoticed when we unloaded our luggage from the cabs. Tuckered out from the travel, he had quietly fallen asleep in the backseat of the car. My parents panicked once they noticed their eldest son was not with the rest of the children. They called the cab company immediately, inquiring about a missing boy. John arrived shortly after their call, yawing, still very tired.

The next day, my sister, Mimi, and I went to visit our neighbors. Delighted with our friendly disposition, they dressed us up in kimonos and wooden slippers. We went home, made up in our new clothes. Mom thought we looked adorable.

Jamal and I used to wake up early in the morning when everyone else was still asleep. He decided to start collecting Japanese stamps. I accompanied him when he left the house to take the neighbor's mail because he liked the way their stamps looked. This went on for a week until he was discovered, to my father's embarrassment. We also loved these little vitamin bottles of Tiger's milk. It was delivered every morning in a small glass bottle with regular large milk in a metal caddy. Our early morning escapade started with drinking some of our neighbors Tiger's milk. As smart as we thought we were, that too came to a quick end.

My parents did not enroll us in school because Dad's assignment was for six months. Mom was thirty-two then with four children, the youngest being me, at six years of age. She kept us busy by taking us to the beach and on our first bullet train, where we had cookies and tea before arriving in Fujisawa to see the Great Buddha of Kamakura.

The four of us used to leave our home and walk down the street to go to the public baths. My sister and I went to the women's side. There was a large floor-to-ceiling tiled wall in the baths, dividing the men's bath from the women's. My sister and I were curious if our brothers were on the other side. In a loud voice, speaking to the wall, we asked our brothers if they were on the other side. We heard them say yes. Our curiosity entertained the women, mostly for breaking the etiquette code of not being silent when bathing. They knew we were new to public baths. Watching foreign children experiencing the Japanese baths for the first time had them giggling.

After arriving in Narita for one day, the children, Scott, and I went to the Naritasan Shinshoji Temple that dates back one thousand years.

I felt reminiscent of my childhood. It was the first time I had been back since 1965. I was elated to share a small piece of Japan with my children. I felt proud of their interest in the Japanese temple tradition, watching them observe, mimicking the Japanese elders. Looking over the bridge, waiting, my children came running to me, insisting that I go into the temple with them. Scott came out to allow me to go in while he watched our bags. My kids asked me to follow them and do exactly as they did. We started by being blessed with incense, and took our shoes off after entering the temple; the children made sure I knew where I needed to place my shoes before we sat on our knees to pray. They sat in front of me, turning around to make sure I knew how to pray by following what they were doing.

The next day we flew out to Guam. After picking up our luggage at the carousel, we headed outside. There was a line of people greeting us, as if we were dignitaries, as we existed the airport entrance. The gentlemen who invited us drove us to the Hyatt Hotel. We had enough time to settle in our presidential suite before meeting everyone downstairs for dinner.

Our host was also our tour guide. He shared many stories with us. The most notable story was about Shōichi Yokoi, a sergeant from the Imperial Japanese Army during WWII. After the U.S. had regained control of Guam in 1944, Shōichi refused to surrender to the American military. Instead he lived in a jungle for 27 years, after which he was discovered and returned to Japan.

Before returning to the United States, we flew to Sydney to snorkel, exploring the Great Barrier Reef. The Cairns Australia Rainforest was right near where we were staying. We took the Skyrail Rainforest Cableway to the rainforest station nature park. As I looked out the window, I noticed that the leaves on the trees were dry; the rainforest was not as lush as I expected.

My mother-in-law had a friend there whom she wanted us to meet up with. His name was Bear. Finding his living quarters in the bush of Tropical North Queensland was not easy. There was no signage, so he gave Scott landmarks to help find his driveway. We pulled up on a dirt road of an abandoned quarry. Scott walked over to Bear to greet him. He seemed a bit stiff. I reminded myself not to be quick to judge someone we were visiting for a moment in time. Oddly, his home did not have any exterior walls. Otherwise, it was fully furnished with rooms, a kitchen, and a bathroom. The guest bathroom was outside a good distance from the main house. It looked like a standard bathroom with a wooden exterior building, mirror, sink, tiled interior, septic plumbing, and a breathtaking panoramic view from a missing door opening. It was my favorite spot, away from a conversation with a man who had a very intense, negative outlook on the future.

On the right side of the house, there was a large, fully-enclosed metal building. We went upstairs to an empty, open room with hardwood floors surrounded by mirrors. He said it was his gym. It did not make any sense to have a workout station in an enclosed building when your home has no exterior walls. I surrendered the notion that this man's life needed to make sense to me. I was just passing by. His wife was a lovely person. I enjoyed our light, cordial exchanges.

It turned out that Bear was Augustus Owsley Stanley III, the infamous LSD chemist soundman who funded the Grateful Dead band from the 1960s. His conversations with us were rigid, paranoid; the future bore gloom and doom. As an easygoing optimist, I find cynical people exhausting. In my opinion, their perspective on life, in general, is usually accompanied by pain from their past.

I was happy to leave Bear's home. Our next stop was Perth, Western Australia, where Jamal was still living.

We rented a place in Rockingham, past Perth, right on the water. I sat on the balcony, watching silhouettes of dolphins swim by in the early mornings. Jamal and I had a week planned together. He was to join us at Margaret River, south of Perth, a gorgeous place for surfers and wine lovers. In California, it would be a Big Sur-Sonoma County cultural fusion. My brother was living with a different woman then. The time he took off from work to be with me was hijacked for her childcare needs. I was extremely disappointed for several reasons. One, he canceled on me. Two, he could have hosted us at his home. It was large enough to house the four of us. His girlfriend would not allow it. He awkwardly apologized to me, knowing that this type of hospitality was a departure from our family values.

The few times I was alone with my brother, we walked to the beach, sat on the sand, reflecting on our lives. We laughed about the silly things we did before we came to the U.S. Jamal said, "Sis, I owe you an apology." "Why?" I asked. "When you were in high school, I made sure no one would ask you out. If they did, I let everyone know that I would beat them up," he said.

"Oh my God, Jamal, that explains all the confusion I felt from the boys I thought liked me."

After Jamal went back to work, we drove down to Margaret River to meet our Californian neighbors. Before moving back to Australia, my neighbor Helen and I became good friends. Our sons played together. They left California to purchase a beautiful flower farm in Margaret River.

We dined at the local winery, picnicked at the beach, caught up on life. My friend suggested we go to the Tree Top Walk on the Valley of the Giants that overlooked an ancient forest, one hundred and thirty-one feet above the ground. We took two cars, heading farther south, then stopped at the magnificent Valley of the Giants to climb the Tree Top Forest. Later that day, we drove to Cape Leeuwin, where the Indian Ocean meets the Southern Ocean in the southernmost part of the Australian continent.

When we returned to Rockingham, we stopped to say goodbye to my brother. He joined us at Freemantle for lunch on our way to the airport. It was unrecognizable from the last time I was there in 1982 when it was still undiscovered. Now, the business community accommodates a much larger, economically diverse population.

Before flying home, we had a two-day layover back in Guam. Looking down from the airplane window, the island looked like a dumpsite. Palm trees entwined with street wires; homes were torn apart. We had just missed a typhoon. The island looked like a landfill as we slowly descended from the sky.

After we disembarked and picked up our luggage, we exited to a city filled with lines of people desperate to escape the island. We checked into our hotel, taking an elevator to our room that stopped at the empty floors.

When the doors opened, we could only see metal structures with cement. All the rooms were completely gutted. One could only imagine where the window framing once stood. Silently, observing the devastation from the typhoon, my mind took note of the structural changes, where the building was most vulnerable.

I distracted the children with snorkeling. Every day we walked through gutted floors filled with international emergency rescue teams. I tried not to react to our circumstances' seriousness. The gas stations were closed. We had no idea if we could leave the island, nor did we know if we could get back to Antonio B. Won Pat International Airport. Scott and I planned to leave early for the airport to give us enough time to walk there should that be our last resort. The front desk called a taxi for us. Waiting for our ride in the lobby after checking out, we were unsure if our possible scenario would take shape—that we might never make it to the airport by taxi. It took the cab two hours to show up after the first call. He said he waited four hours to fill his car tank with gas.

Standing in line to check-in at the airport, we heard echoing stories of people locking themselves up in rooms to survive the typhoon. One man said his whole family all hovered in a small bathroom for safety. It made me wonder what I might have done in their circumstances.

Landing in SFO felt great after being in Guam. We were delighted to be home after a month abroad. The first week back, we had a bad storm, leaving everyone in our community without electricity for seven days unless you had a generator, which we did not.

Months later, Scott and I started remodeling our home. We got into big arguments about the cost of remodeling, with me being the more conservative budgeter. A friend of ours, a contractor, came to speak to us. "Look, people get divorced over remodels all the time," he said. Scott and I already had issues. The remodel was the tip of the iceberg. I was unhappy in my marriage. Our values were changing, and not in the same direction.

For me, it was never about his sexual orientation. Our differences slowly evolved over five years until I requested a divorce.

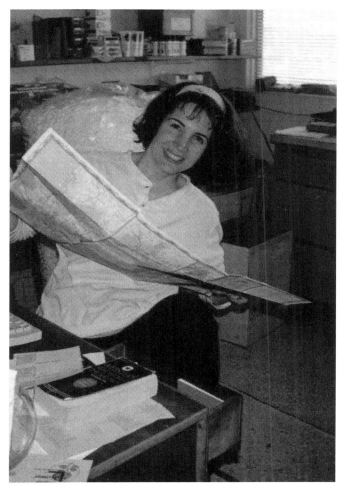

started Sugar Happy Diabetes Supplies from my college apartment

new Sugar Happy storefront

family photo with Scott in Santa Cruz California

Mayor Frank Jordan cuts the ribbon to the store opening in San Francisco

at home in Tokyo Japan

at the train station in Tokyo on our way to see The Great Buddha

at The Great Buddha of Kamakura

at The Naritasan Shinshoji Temple in Narita Japan

children praying in the temple

Jeff's Cove in Gaum with Scott, Spencer and Miranda

Miranda and Spencer at Gun Hill Cannon in Guam

*Skyrail Rainforest Cableway- Barron Gorge National Park, in the Wet
Tropics of Queensland's World Heritage Area*

Bear makes us tea

Spencer learning to start a fire from the Tjapukai Aboriginals

Miranda petting a joey

family photo at a zoo

children snorkeling in Gaum after the typhoon

FROM BAGHDAD TO BERKELEY

Chapter 9
Divorce California Style

Once we decided on the divorce, we had to tell our children, our friends, and our family. The most challenging discussion was with our children. They were nine and ten at the time. I knew that once I that conversation with them, it would mark the end of an era in their life.

Some of our friends were extremely disappointed with the news. They saw us as their marital role models. I told them, "We will still be your role models as divorcees."

My husband and I discussed how to handle the legal dissolution of our assets. Everything we owned we shared equally, including our salaries. We discussed the cost of the divorce, mutually deciding to save money on legal expenses by working with a mediator. Scott found a woman we both liked. As amicable as we were, there were those dark days when our emotions ran deep. The pain, anger, and disappointments were unbearable. The most significant transition when negotiating is moving away from building your assets as a team, to having to make sure your partner does not unfairly divide the accumulated wealth.

Just as we were finalizing a martial settlement agreement, our mediator informed us that she was ill and needed surgery. She prepared all the paperwork for me to take down to the county clerk to file. I needed to have my husband served since I was the one filing for divorce. I called him to explain the process, asking him if I could have a mutual friend of ours serve him. He was agreeable. It took us three hundred sixty-four days from beginning to end to dissolve almost twenty years of our lives.

We went to look at homes to rent for my former husband, to move him out of the back office. The rents we found matched our monthly mortgage payment, so we decided to purchase a home for him instead. I found a house that I thought he would like. He had seen it online and decided against it. I asked him to at least look at it; he did and decided he wanted it. It was up in the hills a few miles from my home. We felt this would be easier for the kids. The school bus stop was near my house; they could walk up the hill or hang out at my home. Their father usually picked them up, unless something came up that prevented him from doing so. My former husband took most of the furniture from our house so the children would feel more settled with familiar belongings in his new home. We continued to take family vacations and celebrated the holidays, birthdays, Mother's Day, and Father's Day together. Sixteen years later, we still do. We did this for the children back then. It wasn't easy for me. As a mother, it is easier for me to place my children's needs above mine.

My former husband and I continued to work as a team together in our business for six more years post-divorce. We developed different visions for the company and could not agree on the direction to keep it viable. Beyond that, Scott was burned out. I bought him out of the company in 2008 when the economy was tanking. It took me ten years to recover financially from the divorce, turning an insolvent business into a profitable one.

I had two friends who were going to France and Italy before my divorce was finalized. One was my best friend from high school, Katherine; my second friend, Joy, was the mother of one of my son's friends from preschool. They both invited me to join them with their families. I took them up on their offer and reached out to my son's former French exchange family from elementary school. Our public school had a standing foreign exchange program with a school in Paris. We hosted a child at our home for three weeks, and our son stayed with his family in France for three weeks. For American children, it was a cultural experience. For French children, it was a language immersion program.

The day before I left for Europe, I accidentally left my debit card at the teller machine. I called the bank, asking them to send a debit card to my hotel in Paris. They said it would be at the hotel upon my arrival. I took extra credit cards to pay for my expenses until my debit card arrived. We boarded Air France from SFO and sat in the last three seats on the right side of the plane. It was a full flight.

The children enjoyed the company of a physicist throughout the flight. His discussion with them kept them captivated. I enjoyed talking to him about quantum physics, debating classical physics versus modern quantum mechanics. Classical physics theory believes that matter is predicable where modern quantum physics believes that matter has a probability component tied to its outcome. It was a treat meeting such an interesting man just as we started our European adventure. At the end of the flight, I thanked the physicist for being so gracious with my children, explaining that it would have been more challenging to keep both of them occupied on a thirteen-hour flight without his help. Watching other parents struggle with their children with less compassionate passengers sitting in front of them made me feel blessed.

After arriving in Paris, we took the train from Charles de Gaulle Airport to our hotel. It was my first solo trip with the kids. A band of Gypsies boarded our Metro compartment. They played music, passing their hat around for tips before moving on to the next cart. I kept the children close to me. We sat on a bench near the exiting door, periodically looking up at the station map, counting the stops to our destination. We checked into the hotel that I booked online. It was in the Montmarte district. The elevator was so small the three of us could not fit our luggage in. I took the kids up to the room first, and then came down to bring up the remaining bags. Exhausted from getting ready for the trip, compounded by the eight-hour time difference, I napped before taking the children out for a walk. I loved Montmarte. I don't speak French, but many people there spoke Arabic. Hailing cabs and dining in restaurants in Arabic made it easier to get around. Nearby was a bumper car venue the children enjoyed. I allowed them to stay on the ride much longer than I usually do. My mind was exhausted. I lost count of how many times the children remained in the car.

The next day we boarded a train with a couchette, a cart with bunk beds for us to sleep in when it was time to go to Tuscany to meet up with Joy. Once it got dark, we pulled down the beds. My children sat crossed-legged on the top bunk with my son teaching his sister how to play chess. I watched them from the lower bunk. It was a sweet moment. My daughter jubilantly exclaimed, "My tooth fell out." To her delight, she was expecting the tooth fairy to visit her from Paris to Pistoia. I needed to be resourceful with the fairy's visit, curious as to when I could slip a few Euros under her pillow.

Gazing at the dark window after the children fell asleep took me back to my overnight train trip when I was fifteen. I left Germany for Holland, sitting uncomfortably on the train for hours. I didn't know they offered sleeping accommodations. There were six people in my compartment. Two couples pulled their seats down to make it into a single bed. I sat across from a young man with a window seat. He looked at me with a questioning face, wondering, if I too, wanted to be more comfortable. He conveyed his thoughts in sign language, gesturing pulling down both seats to make one bed. Sitting on the train became unbearable. The four passengers boxed us in. We awkwardly stepped over each other, turning our seats into a single bed, facing opposite sides. I lay in a fetal position, stretching my legs with a mysterious man on a makeshift bed I would never see again. Oddly, I felt no shame.

In the middle of the night, the border patrol opened the door, turned on the lights, and said, "Passport." I showed them our legal documents. They asked the children to sit up and glanced at their faces, comparing them to their passport photos. A well-dressed African man shared our train accommodations. He showed the men in uniform his passport. They rejected his credentials, continuing with what seemed like an inquisition. The African man opened his passport for the second time, pointing to the information in it, speaking passionately, arguing his position. It frustrated me to see this exchange, wondering if the border patrol was giving him a hard time because of the color of his skin. He had to leave his bunk, pick up his luggage, and walk out in the early morning. I lay there with mixed emotions, reacting to what just transpired— wondering if the guards' actions were justifiable.

After the man left, I slipped a few Euros under my daughter's pillow, feeling relieved that I remembered the tooth fairy's anticipated visit. Shortly afterward, the African man made his way back to his bed.

The next day we arrived in Pistoia. It was a painfully hot day. My friend Joy came to pick us up with her children. The car she had would not start. It was in the afternoon, when the shops were closed. All we could do was walk around until the service garage reopened. A mechanic checked the car out. The minor issue, fixed immediately, allowed us to head to her new home. With record heat, it was the hottest summer Europe had experienced in two hundred years.

Tuscany was beautiful. Joy had traded her home and car with a family who stayed in her California home. We dined in the garden in the evening under a calm, majestic sky. The next day, I went for a morning jog in the countryside. I ran down a narrow dirt road while it was still cool, following the outline of a small vineyard. The grapevines dictated my route, leading me to a small town. I passed a woman who was dressed immaculately in a white-starched apron over her beautiful dress. She looked like she belonged on a Disney movie set, sweeping her front porch. As I jogged by her, she stopped to stare at me. Shortly after I passed her, someone came out on their balcony to watch me. It continued this way until I ran through the town. Every morning I jogged around the same time along the same route. My audience started multiplying. More people would stand in the street, outside their front door or balcony to watch me pass by. Some were sipping their coffee in bathrobes, looking down at me. I spontaneously glanced up, noticing their presence. To counter my uncomfortable feelings, I kept chanting, "I am normal, I am normal," as I jogged by the gawkers.

One day, we decided to take a day trip to Florence. Walking through the historical center, the children and I walked to the Piazza del Duomo, Piazza dei Ciompi, and then the famous Florence Flea Market. The locals displayed the most unusual collection of chess sets, made from metal and stone. My son bought a slingshot and a leather jacket. My daughter purchased a personalized apron with Italian text and a wallet.

Later during the week, my friend took us to an outdoor pool surrounded by the Tuscan hills. My daughter jumped into the water to swim. My son sat next to me. Overtaken by bliss, I felt grateful to be lounging by the gorgeous hills that engulfed us—these memories were for me. My children were too young to remember the daily details of our Tuscan visit. It reminded me of my peaceful family vacation frolicking in the pool in Lebanon, surrounded by a breathtaking view, before arriving in the U.S.

During my stay in Tuscany, both our families decided to go to Venice for a three-day trip. Getting to the Pistoia train station took two car trips from the house. The car could not seat us all. We checked the train schedule to allocate enough time to make the two trips to the station. Adding to the usual stress when traveling, a running event started at the bottom of the mountain en route to my friend's home. Joy stayed focused. Unfazed by the foot traffic, she successfully got us all to the train station on time.

Once we got there, the man behind the ticket booth would not sell us tickets. My friend Joy was very calm. The seven of us stood behind her while she thumbed through her Italian dictionary, trying to understand what the man was saying. I was a bit scared; the ticket clerk raised his voice when he spoke to us, angrily stood up from his chair, pushed it back with a sudden aggressive move, and walked away from his desk as if he was going to leave through the side door to explode. He refused to sell us tickets with no rational explanation.

An African woman, who was fluent in Italian and English, stepped in to help us. She raised her voice, arguing on our behalf, threatening the man behind the glass window by calling the police if he did not sell us tickets. He begrudgingly gave us our tickets. She later told us he did not want to sell us tickets because he felt we were "stupid Americans who could not speak Italian. It was not nice of him," she added.

It took us a bit over three hours to get to Venice. Joy's husband played chess with the boys. Exiting the train station to the Piazza in Venice was spectacular. We caught a water taxi to get to our hotel. I instantly fell in love with Venice. It took me back to my high school days when we studied Roman mythology. Taxiing through the waterways, I imagined how the Roman Gods must have lived in such a breathtaking city.

We checked into our beautiful rooms. I was still trying to connect with my bank for my debit card. My friend offered to watch the kids while I went downstairs to the restaurant to call. It took many calls. The restaurant closed while I waited for the bank to call me back. A young man who worked at the hotel approached me. He looked at my shoes, then me, and said in a thick Italian accent, "Those look like men's shoes." Uncertain as to how I should respond, I just looked at my green loafers, then him. He came closer, lifted my left foot, took my shoe off, and said, "I think you need a foot massage."

I pulled my foot from his hands, reached down, picked up my shoe, and put it back on. "Thank you for your offer. But I do not need a massage," I responded. This incident forced me to abandon my hope of reaching my bank.

The heat was unbearable in Venice. We discovered Orangina to quench our thirst, gelato to cool our temperature, and outdoor casual dining areas for a light summer meal. In the piazza, we saw people dressed in Carnival costumes. I saw glass blowing, discovering Moreno glass. We walked through the Jewish Ghetto, exploring art galleries. The three days went by quickly. On our way back to the train station, we stood outside while the children cooled themselves in the front entrance sprinklers.

It was wonderful to share a family vacation with Joy. I have always enjoyed our conversations. She is honest, reflective, intellectual, and adventurous.

The children and I made our way back to Paris. It was time to meet up with my best friend from high school, Katherine. She made our reservation at a quaint boutique hotel near the opera house. I checked in at the front desk, and asked if they had a package for me. To my disappointment, no debit card. It continued to be an inconvenience throughout my travels.

I enjoyed being with my best friend from high school with our children, something we never dreamt of and appreciated thoroughly. We visited Napoleon Bonaparte's tombstone, and walked around the city of Paris to the Eiffel Tower. Later, we went to the Arc de Triomphe, wined, dined, and shopped until our weary bodies dropped on our beds.

I received the news that my father was quite ill. Concerned that he might pass away, I called my former husband to ask him if it would be okay to take the children to Baghdad, Iraq. I explained that this might be the last opportunity for them to meet their grandfather. In the 1990s, Iraq was a warzone. There never seemed to be a good time to take the children there to meet my family and experience the life as I had as a child.

In 2003, Saddam was in hiding. Scott said he was uncomfortable with the idea, but he understood that this might be the last time I would see my father. We discussed how the kids would return to the U.S. without me. He was happy to pick them up from the airport. He missed having them home.

We scheduled a day to visit my son's French exchange family in Paris. Fabienne, the mother, made a delicious quiche for lunch. We chatted, discussing how much we loved each other's boys and how difficult it was to have them leave after their programs ended. I mentioned that I was going to go to Baghdad, then return to Paris for a work conference. She offered me her flat. She planned to be in the countryside upon my return.

Katherine's days in Paris were coming to an end. With the flight attendant's oversite, I changed my children's departure date to board a direct flight back to San Francisco without me. Their father picked them up at the airport. I then purchased a direct flight to Jordan.

The night before my children were to board the plane, all my siblings called to ask me not to go to a warzone for a family visit. I explained that I felt safe and knew what to do. They pleaded with me. Each one ended the conversation with, "I know once you have made up your mind, nothing will change it."

As the evening progressed, I got very sick. I laid in bed, holding my stomach, shivering, feeling cold, then running to the bathroom to throw up. Katherine happened to stop by and saw my ailing condition. She had me get in a hot bath. Concerned with how ill I was, I asked if she could take the children to the airport for me. The next day, upon her return, I rolled in bed with continued discomfort, I asked her how it went. She said that the kids were distracted at the train station, and the airport security would not let her walk the children to the gate because she was not the parent. In the end, after many frustrating discussions with the airport crew, it all worked out. I thanked her for all she had done.

Regardless of my illness, the front desk called my room every day, asking me to leave. I continued to be sick for several days past my checkout time. Katherine argued with the management, telling them they could not kick me out when I could not walk. The disagreement continued until she insisted that I stay in her room with her. Fortunately, her teenage daughter had a separate room. The hotel manager kept checking in on me after I moved. Katherine had run out for an errand when management came by knocking on the door. I staggered to unlock the room in my nightgown. When the manager saw how ill I was; he sent up a breakfast tray, apologizing for disturbing me.

Three days after the first incident, I felt much better. Katherine returned to America. I boarded a plane to Jordan. I heard through the grapevine that to get to Baghdad through Jordan, I needed to hire a driver with gunmen to enter Iraq. Driving from the Jordanian border to Baghdad was extremely dangerous. Saddam was in hiding. He released all the prisoners, making the roads unsafe to travel. The streets were no longer safe. Cars were being pulled over at gunpoint to be robbed.

In the Middle East, people carry cash and gold, which are hard assets, valuable to many. After checking into a hotel, I started inquiring about hiring a driver with armed men to taxi me to Baghdad. The front desk asked me to return later. I called my father. No one answered. I then called my uncle to tell him about my plans. He asked me to allow him to arrange a ride for me. A former engineer who made medical supply runs from Amman to Baghdad picked me up with a rough-looking man who appeared to have a military background.

When I went online in Paris to search "Visa for Iraq," the U.S. State Department's advisory bulletin did not recommend visiting Iraq. If anything happened, there were no guarantees the American military or diplomatic corps could assist me in any way. If I wanted to apply for a visa, it would take weeks and an HIV test. I did not have that much time on my hands and decided to take my chances at the Jordanian border. I counted on my last name and birthplace, as stated in my U.S. passport, to circumvent the standard border protocol for getting through.

I dozed off in the backseat until we arrived at the Iraqi border. Earlier, my driver instructed me not to speak Arabic when crossing the Jordan border. The guard turned on his flashlight to check the backseat through the dark window. Feeling sleepy, I was too tired to do anything except nod as instructed. My driver told the guard that my father was ill. My visit to Iraq was to spend time with my sick father before his passing. After five minutes, we crossed over to Iraq.

I was eager to view a place I once called home. All my previous visits there were under my parent's rein. I felt curious about how I would feel meeting my family again after a twenty-five-year absence. We drove through the desert. A magnificent sunrise, larger than life, low on the horizon with bright orange hues, dominated a calm sandy desert. Reminiscent of my childhood excavating outings, I asked the driver to pull over. The taxicab driver accommodated me with fascination. I could see my request struck him. He also had a schedule and wanted to keep the stops to a minimum. I jumped out of the car to take a photo, capturing a familiar feeling that once was a symbol of home.

Mesmerized by the sunrise driving through the desert, I reflected on my mother's life in the Middle East with a new appreciation of what it must have been like for her to move there in 1955. It reminded me that not everyone seeks adventure or is open to learning about another civilization to embrace. Mom did not reside in familiarity. With no expectations, she married an elite foreigner at the age of nineteen.

Her ability to appreciate other cultures marked a life full of travel and adventure. It's something that she passed down to me. I could see a smile on her face, feel her love, as we drove through the desert. It was as if we were meeting across all dimensions, sharing an illusion where no time had elapsed since her passing in 2000, the day before Valentine's Day. Both my parents had a mischievous smile when I shared my personal stories with them, validating my defiance. It could be that I reminded them of a younger version of themselves.

My driver was extremely entertaining. He picked my brain to see how he could marry an American woman. Knowing that he already has an Iraqi wife, I explained that polygamy is not legal in the U.S., like it is in Muslim countries. He couldn't grasp the concept. I kept shooting down his varying scenarios of how he could circumvent the American laws to add an American wife to his marital status.

My uncle came to greet me as we pulled into his driveway. I loved him and his wife dearly. The family driver of thirty years greeted me from the kitchen on my way to the living room. We sat in the living room, sipping tea with my three cousins who were much younger than me. We caught up on family and work matters. It was late in the afternoon when my uncle dropped me off at my father's house.

My dad was delighted and surprised to see me at his home in Baghdad. We had engaging conversations catching up on life in America. He was proud of me for building a business up from the ground floor. I met my other half-siblings. One of my sisters was to be married in three weeks. My father moved the wedding up a week so that I could be there. It allowed me to experience the traditions a new bride goes through in a Muslim marriage.

One night, while sitting at dinner with the whole family, my father asked about my mother's passing. He needed something back in 2000 from one of the siblings, but he could not remember which American child he had asked. I told him it was me. He asked me why I did not deliver what he needed to honor my mother's passing in Baghdad. I said,

"Dad, I did not send that to you because it was from a different time in your life. You have a new family. Out of respect for your new wife, I felt it was best not to do so."

"You should have sent me what I requested," he said, and left the table.

I was excited to see my cousins, whom I spent a lot of time with when I attended the University of Baghdad. They were all married with children now. Some were abroad living in France and Saudi Arabia. Two of my cousins were still in Baghdad. I went to visit and spend the night with one of them. She worked for the United Nations. In my honor, she hosted a family party for me, inviting many family members. To both of our surprise, some who have not spoken to each other in decades attended.

Standing in the kitchen as people were still arriving, my cousin looked me and said, "Nadia, your visit is changing our family history. Look at how many people who have not spoken to each other in decades are attending."

"It makes me happy," I responded.

My cousin's birthday was the next day. I wanted to take her shopping to buy her a birthday gift. She worked half a day and came home during lunch. I was ready to go. But just before leaving, my cousin asked me if I would mind waiting until after lunch. She went to prepare lunch in the kitchen while I sat in the family room. We heard a big explosion in front of the house. Although I had no previous experience as an adult in a warzone, I knew a bomb had gone off. My cousin and I called one another to make sure we were safe. I ran to the front of the house and was surprised the building was still standing. I slowly pulled the curtains back from the living room window; I could see seven American soldiers in the front with guns pointed at us, resting their rifles between the concrete and metal fence. My cousin's children were upstairs, pulling the curtains back from their rooms. I felt like a sitting duck, vulnerable to be being helplessly shot. I quickly realized that the soldiers thought we had set off the bomb. Critical mass came to mind, as when cyclists stick together for their safety on the roads. I hollered in Arabic to the family, "Let's all go to the family room and let the soldiers come to us." I paced, tears came to my eyes, fearing that my children may become motherless. I was determined to make it back for them.

My cousin went to peek out of the kitchen window, next to the family room. "Nadia, the Americans are coming, the Americans are coming," she hollered in a stressed voice. "Come to speak to them."

From the right side of the house, we slowly opened the kitchen door single file, exiting one by one with our arms up in the air, with me being in the front of the line. Fortunately, we were all women and children. Seven young soldiers stood in front of us with their guns cocked, hands shaking, ready to shoot. Their index fingers were sitting on the triggers. We were all scared. Looking into the soldier's eyes, I knew their fear could cause them to pull the trigger without even meaning to. The soldiers had a "one-shot" rule where they could pull the trigger once without asking any questions. I did not know if it meant all seven of them could shoot once or one person from the squad could shoot once. My survival mechanism kicked in. My mind searched for the shortest syllable word to let the soldiers know that I am American.

"Hi," I said in an unrecognizable octave. The soldier in charge asked, "You are American?" "Yes," I replied. Things started moving quickly. He explained that he was in a Humvee on patrol when a bomb detonated in the middle of the road. A remote control was used, from what they assumed was our location, setting off the bomb. A young Iraqi translator accompanied them. I told him to "be quiet" in Arabic. "I will translate now." If looks could kill, I was dead. Women do not tell men to be quiet in Baghdad.

My cousin's mother-in-law lived next door in the same compound. The sergeant asked me a series of questions. I turned to my cousin to ask her for her answers. She responded in Arabic. I answered the sergeant in English. "Did you notice anything outside that was unusual?" he asked. I turned to my cousin, who stood behind me, to ask her the same questions in Arabic.

"Is there anyone on the roof right now?" I answered, "No." The questions and answers were quick-paced, intense. At one point, I asked my cousin a question in Arabic, turned to the American sergeant, and answered it in Arabic. Realizing my error, I paused, and we all started laughing. It broke the life-threatening tension we felt.

The American soldiers filed into my cousin's mother-in-law's home. They moved quickly, running in, stopping, turning from side to side, hiding, and pointing their guns with their hand on the trigger before advancing. They cleared both homes. The sergeant asked, "Where are you from?"

"California," I responded.

"You are a long way from home," he said. "What brought you to Baghdad?" he asked.

"I came to visit my ailing father," I replied.

The soldiers sectioned off the street to interrogate the rest of the people and businesses outside my cousin's home. We all went back into the house, relieved we survived a bombing with only an interrogation. I sat in the family room, trying to process what happened when I heard my cousin scream in another shrieking sound. "Nadia, the Americans have Mohamed! Come speak to them!" This time, I knew who I was dealing with.

"Hey," I screamed out from a distance, staring at the soldiers that had a gun on my cousin's son's head. "Why are you holding a gun to his head?" I asked.

"He is taking photos of the area," he said.

"That is my camera," I said. "I have pictures of my children from France and Italy that I want to keep. I can delete any images you want me to from my camera, but you are not taking it away." I scrolled through the photos until the serviceman was satisfied.

The biggest disappointment for me in Baghdad was to learn that some American soldiers loot innocent people's valuables when invading a suspected home. I naively believed that all deployed American soldiers were honest, representing our democratic justice system.

That evening, my uncle threw a party for me. It was a family party. He and my father, my uncle's only living brother, had their disagreements for decades. Unfortunately, they litigated in court over the family's assets. However, my father never forbade me from having a relationship with his siblings. Regardless of their legal standing, I came and went to family functions.

My cousin and I dressed up for the party. We were still shell-shocked, feeling numb, going through the motions at my uncle's party, taking photos with different family members. I spoke to Scott that night on the roof of the penthouse. My cousin's children were running around with sticks, waving them, playing. American helicopters flew over the Tigris River above me. I asked the children to go inside, fearing their waving bats may be misinterpreted by the military flight, signaling a defense strategy.

I was crying on the phone, reflecting on how our children could have been motherless. I asked to speak to the children. I could tell by their tone they were scared for me. I felt terrible because I could not hold them to assure them that I was okay.

My Iraqi sister's fiancé came over before their wedding to socialize with us. He was a nice young man. My sister felt inhibited, understandably so. She would get to know him after their marriage.

On the day of a Muslim wedding, the men and women are segregated and socialize in different rooms. Most of the women belly dance after the couple ties the knot. The groom has the privilege of staying in the room when the women are dancing.

Before leaving Iraq, my cousin took me to the Palestinian district to buy original art. I especially liked several pieces by the same artist. After I purchased artwork from the gallery, the owner wrapped up the canvases for me to carry on the plane.

The night before I left, I knew this would be the last time I would see my father. We stayed up all night. I interviewed him. "Dad, which football team is your favorite?" "The 49ers," he said.

"I remember seeing my first game in San Francisco with Jimmy and Harry, your mother's Irish cousins, who took me to Kezar Stadium."

"What about baseball?" I asked. "The Giants," he responded.

"As a dignitary, you traveled the world. Which city was your favorite city?" I asked.

"Stockton," he replied. I realized he must have loved Stockton because of my Aunt Miriam and Uncle Rex. He was feeling sentimental. Stockton is not a tourist destination.

"Dad, what is your biggest regret in life?" I asked.

"The divorce. I never wanted it. Your mother did." That silenced me.

My father added that he wrote a letter that my brother in Iraq has. Upon his passing, my half-brother was to give it to me. It was related to our inheritance.

My half-brother insisted on chaperoning me to the Jordanian border with his wife. A cab driver picked us up early in the morning. It was another bittersweet moment. Like when I left Bibi, my grandmother, I knew this would be the last time I would see my dad. Out of all of his kids, we had a unique relationship that none of my other siblings shared.

The cab driver was reckless on the roads. I commented on his driving in Arabic after my head hit the car's interior the third time. He didn't realize I was serious in criticizing his driving. He laughed as if it was a joke. The ride was unnecessarily jerky. I hung on to the safety strap that was dangling from above my window.

We approached the Jordanian border. There were rows and rows of vehicles at a stop. I guessed at least two hundred cars were waiting to get through. Our driver asked us if we wanted to bribe the guard. My brother and I said "no" in unison. The Iraqi guard walked up to our vehicle. The driver rolled down his window and then proceeded to bribe the guard, asking him to advance us through the border for a large tip. The guard was rightfully upset. He asked us to get out of the car and detained us until his higher-up authorities could speak to us in a private room. We stood in a long line. A Sheik, a man who is the head of his tribe, walked into the office, passing us without waiting.

After speaking to the patrolling guard in one office, they sent me to another office to evaluate the artwork I had purchased. My brother stayed close to me. The guards unrolled the artwork, studied it in detail, and looked for any signs that might indicate valuable artwork was being smuggled across the border. They kept me in their office for one hour, then charged me a two-hundred-and-fifty-dollar tax, which I knew they would pocket.

We continued to stand around for another two hours. I saw a very tall German man whom, for whatever reason, I thought must be a spy. He seemed to share my thought of him, thinking I was an American spy. Next to me was a woman in jeans wearing open-toe Birkenstocks. She had to be American. I walked up to her, introduced myself, and asked her where she was from. "Harlem, New York," she answered. I asked her what brought her to Baghdad during a war. She said she was a nun, part of an order who came to Baghdad to look for missing Iraqi family members.

The tall German man kept an eye on me. I reciprocated his suspicious gesture. We all left the border within thirty minutes of one another. Relieved to be in Jordan, I now knew I would make it home. We drove for several hours before we stopped to eat at one restaurant. I walked in with my brother and sister-in-law. A person greeted us and pointed to a table she was going to seat us at. Walking through the restaurant, I saw the tall German man. We acknowledged each other's presence without saying a word to each other.

My brother had me dropped off first in Amman before going to meet up with his wife's family. I went to check in at the hotel desk. The tall German man was checking in before me. He turned around after he got his keys and saw me. We looked right at each other, and said nothing. Coincidence? I don't know. I was too tired to think about anything else. I went to my room and fell asleep right away. The next day I woke up, put on my jeans and a shirt, went downstairs, grabbed the *Wall Street Journal*, and sat down at a table for breakfast. I looked up, and who was sitting across from me? The tall German man. I didn't know what to think of this anymore. Was I traveling through a popular route, stopping at a popular restaurant, staying at a popular hotel?

That evening, my cousin, who was living in Saudi Arabia, visited me at my hotel in Amman. We stayed up late, talked, and caught up. After she left, I returned to my room. My uncle called me on the phone to ask where I was that evening. I told him about my cousin visiting me. "Where is she staying?" he asked. I gave him the name of her hotel. "How long did you talk for?"

"For hours. We had a lot to catch up on," I said.

"Why? Do you think I am at the bar, drinking, talking to men?" I asked. He changed the topic and informed me of what time we were to meet the next day at his apartment.

My last day in Amman, my uncle took me to the airport. I kissed him on the cheek and gave him a big goodbye hug. When I turned to wave goodbye before I stepped off the escalator onto the next floor, a guard asked me a question in Arabic. I understood almost everything he asked. In an Iraqi accent, I told him I did not know what one word meant. "What do you mean you do not understand that word?" he asked in his Jordanian accent. He was frustrated with me. Maybe he thought I was playful. He let me pass to board my plane.

I flew Air France back to Paris, arriving at Charles de Gaulle airport. I had no accommodations planned. Exhausted after having fetched my luggage and finding a hotel before going to my son's French family's apartment, I felt impatient. I wanted to scream, have a temper tantrum. The most straightforward task required more patience than I had. Feeling relieved to be outside a warzone, I held everything in until I felt safe enough to unleash my suppressed emotions. In retrospect, I was exhibiting early signs of PTSD; I felt anxious, with few coping mechanisms to deal with post-bombing decision-making.

A person at the airport helped me find a hotel. I took a cab there. After checking in, I had no plans to leave. I purchased fruit and yogurt, and sat in my room for two days. Lying in bed, I could see people, cars, and police through my window. I found a new appreciation for an infrastructure that kept citizens safe from one another. My will to leave the room was gone. I laid there for forty-eight hours, processing my two-week trip, playing back the events, and reliving them. My mind could not rest.

My son's French family was incredibly gracious in offering their home upon my return. They were in the countryside. The wife's brother met me at their apartment to give me the keys to their flat. I had left my luggage with them before leaving for Baghdad. I had purchased a small duffle bag in France so that I could travel with just a few things in case I had to run, averting anything from political unrest to roadside bandits. The bombing was not how I imagined things would play out.

I caught the Metro to the Porte de la Villette stop. After picking up my press pass at the convention center, I entered the conference and walked around to see which American companies were launching in Europe. I struggled with being there. I couldn't tell if it was the time difference or emotional exhaustion. Shortly after the conference ended, I flew back to San Francisco, returning to my ordinary life.

My children ran through the front door after the school bus dropped them off. I could feel their relief for my safety in their long-awaited hug. My father's gifts segued into a light dialogue I had with my children about New Baghdad. The presents were from the district my grandfather built, a token of my lineage they would never learn to know. They saw photos of family members at feasts, with smiling faces in foreign garb, with no emotional ties. It felt safe to be home again.

The next day, I woke up early, and went out to my orchard to work. Families that I knew drove by, stopped, and got out of their cars to tell me how relieved they were I was home. They called me a hero. I found this a bit embarrassing, unsure why I was a hero. In my absence, my former husband shared my stories with our community.

Someone once asked me, what was my one take away from Baghdad. "Surrender," I said. After standing in front of seven soldiers with cocked guns ready to shoot at the slightest move, knowing that I could not control the outcome, I had to accept my fate. Letting go, trusting what I needed to do next, expecting the worst and hoping for the best.

divorce family vacation in the Dominican Republic

first day in Paris with the children

in Paris with Spencer and Miranda

dinner with Katherine in Paris

Spencer teaches Miranda how to play chess on the train on our way to Tuscany

Spencer and Miranda in Venice on a water taxi

Spencer and Miranda at the Florence Flea Market

in front of the Duomo Cathedral in Florence

bombed at my cousin's home

dancing at my sister's wedding

purchasing art in the Palestinian district in Baghdad

dad and I inside the Al-Samarrie Mosque

top right-Cousin Jimmy Cook introduces my father to his first football game at Kezar Stadium in San Francisco, Cousin Diane, mom, Great Aunt Mary, Spencer and I

FROM BAGHDAD TO BERKELEY

Chapter 10
Recovery

Eight months after returning from the Baghdad bombing and still meditating over my divorce, I decided to further decompress by going to Maui with a girlfriend. I rented a beautiful cottage that overlooked an orchard in Maekawa in the countryside of the island. The roads reminded me of Northern California, narrow streets with an endless formation of trees that led me up a road with few visible homes.

Before heading to our house, we stopped at the Manna health food store to stock up on groceries. In broad daylight, it was easy to find the front gate to the accommodations. The four-wheel-drive climbed a broken dirt road surrounded by trees. The foliage brushed the car's windshield when driving downhill to the cottage that overlooked the orchard.

It took us a day to settle in after putting away our groceries, sitting on the high porch overlooking the fruit trees. Every morning we made over-easy eggs and red potato home fries, with strongly brewed Kona coffee. Sitting on the deck was peaceful. Now and then, my mind couldn't help but wander to the warzone. Emotions flooded my psyche, reliving, surviving the bombing, and just like a light switch, my mind crossed over realities to the peaceful orchard.

My friend had a client who wanted us to go whale watching on a unique cruise that mostly locals went on. The next day we met her friend at the dock early to board the boat. February is a great time to whale watch in Hawaii when the humpback whales migrate to the warm Hawaiian waters. I wore my tankini under a dress, placing a sarong in my purse for later. Thirty minutes after we pulled away from the dock, the captain came on the speaker to thank everyone on board for choosing his cruise line. He then informed all the nudists that they could now unclothe if they wish. This most certainly was one of those Chevy Chase movie moments. Less than eight months ago, I was veiled in the Middle East for my safety. Now I sat with a bunch of nudists and a Tantric teacher, a naked woman walking around the boat offering ginger snacks on a silver platter for people who were feeling motion sickness.

The captain stopped the boat after he spotted a pod of whales. Naked men and women jumped into the ocean with snorkels and flippers to swim. I sat on the top deck with my sarong covering my head and shoulders like a hijab watching a sea of bopping naked butts snorkeling. The woman who invited us to this unique venture took her top off and walked around the boat half-naked. I looked up to the sky in silence and shook my head side to side, saying, "God, you have a great sense of humor." I laughed out loud on the empty deck.

Nudists make me feel like a prude. At the same time, I am okay with doing what is most comfortable for me, knowing I will be judged regardless of what I do. I am either cool like them or a prude unlike them. I don't feel freer to be unclothed. My public preference is to be clothed. For some people being naked offers an element of freedom, or overcoming judgments and fear. I get it, even though I do not share their sentiment.

The hot sun's reflection against the water magnified the heat. To cool down, my friend and I decided to get into the ocean. We headed down the steps to the back of the boat and used a ladder to get into the water. I had an eerie feeling that something was beneath us. When I looked down towards the ocean floor, I saw bubbles surfacing. It was both hypnotic and paralyzing. We floated facedown mesmerized by the ball of lights. I didn't notice that the boat drifted far away from us.

Feeling uncomfortable with the distance and worried the captain might forget us, we started to swim towards the boat. The ocean waters created resistance. We stroked forward with an eye on the boat ahead. It took more energy to catch up than we had anticipated. We boarded the boat tired of the long-distance afternoon swim. People told us that we were very close to the whales. I wondered if the white bubbles we saw were the humpbacks circling below.

After Maui and my divorce, I decided to join a relationship group. Our therapist, Steve whom I met at the Spirit Rock Meditation Center, limited the group to three men and three women. I first had to interview with him before being accepted into the next phase. Once he felt I would be a good addition to the group, he questioned the other participants about how they felt about me. When asked why I wanted to join a relationship group by my peers, I said, "I wanted to know what it was like to be with a heterosexual man. My former husband is a gay man who is emotionally intelligent. What I have experienced with heterosexual men is that most men do not know what they want. Sometimes they will settle with a person who may not be the most suitable partner, fearing to be alone for the rest of their lives."

I, on the other hand, have girlfriends with whom I share a strong emotional bond. Generally, men rely heavily on their one female partner to meet all their emotional needs. Women typically have a group of women they count on to help them sort through their conflicting feelings. Unlike men, some women, like myself, don't fear to be alone.

One year before the holidays, our therapist took a break. He went to India to the Oneness Center to become a Deeksha Blessing Giver, commonly known as the Oneness Blessing. After returning from his trip, he asked us if we would like to experience what he learned. The group said yes. He instructed us to close our eyes and focus on breathing, to get into a meditative state. He then put his hands on each one of our heads for two minutes. Afterward, we all shared how calm we felt from our blessing. We started getting a Deeksha Blessing before and after our group session.

What I observed about the group pre-blessing ritual is that some people were a bit short and intolerant. That slowly came to an end, fading away so we no longer had to process adversarial feelings. The discussions we started to have become more generative, less judgmental. We even went out as a group a few times.

I asked our therapist how I could become a "Blessing Giver." He told me I needed to go to India to the Oneness University for a three-week silent retreat. Before I left, I needed to be vegan for three months.

Although I had been in a warzone, India still seemed a scary place in my mind. The only reference I had to the country was the loss of one of my male friends, never to be found again after his visit. My childhood best friend also became deathly ill when visiting India. Her family wasn't sure if she would survive what she contracted on her stay there. The Oneness University offered a chaperone who would take us to our spiritual retreat. My safety was my biggest concern.

I applied for a ten-year visa to India. The form I completed asked the purpose of my trip and my profession. I answered silent spiritual retreat at the Oneness University and Publisher/Journalist in the diabetes industry. My visa was declined. The Indian Embassy was only willing to offer me a short-term six-month visa because of my profession. Additionally, I had to sign a document stating that I would not film or write during my stay.

I left San Francisco Airport in March of 2007 with a layover in Changi Singapore, which is considered one of the best airports in the world. Inside is a beautiful little city with green vegetation, a waterfall, a hotel with beds travelers can rent by the hour, showers, massage stations, and manicure and pedicure salons that both men and women frequented. I had a sixteen-hour layover. Unsure of how to book a bed online at the airport, I decide to request a room when I got there. The woman at the front desk said they were sold out of beds for the next eight hours. This

left me roaming the airport for lo
Eventually, it became unbearable un
the Transit Hotel. The next day I fo
free guided bus tour. With time to sp
flight to India, I checked in with th
passport, boarded a luxury bus, and
educational tour. Chewing gum is illeg
and dispose of it by throwing it on the s
Littering, jaywalking, and smoking in ___ are prohibited. Same-sex
relations are not allowed. It may be hard for Americans to fathom, but
when the government has a surplus in income, Singapore refunds the
excess to its population. The amount you receive is based on your annual
salary.

The demographics changed significantly at the airport when it was
time to board the plane to India. As a single, Caucasian woman traveling
alone, I stood out.

Arriving in Chennai on a hot, humid evening in March of 2007 in
a densely populated city felt courageous considering my preconceived
fears. People looked at me as a foreigner. I looked at them, feeling like a
foreigner, unsure how I would be received. I hailed a cab to take me to
the hotel where I was spending one night, before I met up with my group
the next day. The taxi dropped me off at 11 pm. The man at the front
desk informed me he did not have a reservation for me. I insisted that he
did by handing over my email confirmation for my reservation. He told
me that my email was an error, and refused to give me a room for the
evening. Yet, he made room for a family who walked in inquiring about
accommodations. Feeling uncomfortable with venturing out to look for
a new hotel at night in a city with a population of nearly seven million, I
dug in my feet and refused to leave. I stood in the lobby for one hour,
insisting on a room that I had already paid for online. Exhausted from
our verbal exchanges, the man finally agreed to give me a room.

rved only one night at this particular hotel. I couldn't

early to depart.

e next day, I left minutes after waking, and rolled my luggage
n a dusty street. Young women dressed in saris looked at me. I
struggled to push my luggage with wheels on the bumpy dirt road to a
paved street to hail a ride. Unlike the night before, I felt more confident
navigating my way in daylight. A rickshaw picked me up. On our way to
my destination, we came to a roundabout with heavy morning traffic.
There were many cars, a man walking a cow, a family of four on a
motorcycle, a bicyclist, and myself in a rickshaw all converging at the same
time. It was too stressful to watch. I closed my eyes, took a deep breath,
then opened them, hoping no one had collided.

I arrived at the meeting point early enough to go window-shopping.
I walked around Spencer Mall, admiring all the silk goods for sale.
Sightseeing, I couldn't help but notice tin shacks lined up near the water
that served as homes.

Later that morning, students heading to the Oneness University
started milling around the pickup point. I knew two people, one from
California and one from Maui, who also signed up for the same
program—seeing their familiar faces provided relief. They were my
connection to my life outside of India. The leader of the group checked
all the names off her list.

We boarded a beautiful, air-conditioned bus with comfortable seats
designed to carry large groups on long journeys. The drive to the
university through high traffic areas brought the bus to a halt in traffic
jams. Gazing out the window, I caught a glance of a tall, slender,
impoverished woman carrying a large basket on her head. She looked
right at me, giving me a heartfelt smile. The state of peace she emanated
was confusing to me. I am embarrassed to say that as the women glanced

at me with a sincere smile, I was thinking that I would be miserable if I had to live that way.

After checking in at the Oneness Center, one of the women who I spoke to at the bus station before boarding the bus ended up being one of my nine roommates. Her bed was next to mine. On the first day of our silent retreat, I woke up early, and put on my jogging clothes to run circles on the dirt road for thirty minutes before breakfast. The compound was locked. Men and women were segregated into two buildings. No one could leave the compound without being escorted. Every morning, I placed thirteen drops of grapefruit seed oil in a glass of water to drink before eating breakfast, something I read that was supposed to prevent getting sick when traveling in India. There were a few western items for breakfast, but for the most part, all the meals were Indian cuisine.

I arrived early at the mediation center, placing my adjustable floor mat on the right side of the aisle, the designated space for the women. I was told that these silent retreats are usually segregated by gender. But this particular year, they did not have enough attendees to have two sessions.

There was a large table in the center of the front room, serving as an altar for us to place photos of family members we wanted to pray for. People from all religious backgrounds filled the room. Our group was comprised of Christians, Muslims, Jews, Buddhists, and Hindus. Our teachers, the Dasas, similar to an order of monks or nuns, were extremely young compared to the mature students in the audience. The leadership started the class by addressing the Westerner's bias on young adults being accepted as wise spiritual leaders. They explained that our Dasas might be in their twenties, but they have studied under a spiritual leader for fourteen years.

The program started with a discussion of how relationships are paramount to living. As humans, our relationships with others are what shape us. We cannot live isolated lives and be happy. A world void of relationships is nonexistent. The decisions we make as mature adults result from the choices we have made as children or young adults. For example, if I failed at something when I was younger, or was repeatedly told by someone that I am not good at something, I could adopt the thought process that I will never get this, so why try? I could give up, depriving myself of the opportunity of ever being good at it.

We learned about a process where we can see our thoughts without our ego being involved. If I think about being enlightened or what it means, I am not in the state of Enlightenment. Being detached from the thought process, seeing a story without an emotional, intellectual, or physical reaction is Enlightenment— a peaceful, detached state.

The class started at 8 am every morning with a blissful mediation. Sometimes it ended at midnight. Mediation on these days involved eight hours of going within ourselves, dedicating ourselves to going deep into understanding our pain, releasing hurtful memories, learning to observe ourselves compassionately, searching for the root of our pain, and confronting judgmental familial voices that intentionally or unintentionally hurt us. The process is meant to help one come to peace with their demons, retiring the echoing voice of self-doubt and the conversations we have with ourselves in silence that prevent us from pursuing our dreams to define what makes us happy. What influences the way we think? Our upbringing, family, social conditioning, and society's expectations are what rob us from our happiness.

Anytime I share lodging with people, someone will cross my path who will bring up issues for me. I had this happen with a German woman at the Oneness Center. Every time I saw her in the bathroom area brushing her teeth, getting ready in the morning, I had hostile feelings towards her. It confused me. I knew it could not be her. But something about her made me feel uneasy every time I saw her. It took me weeks to figure it out. Feeling ashamed for my strong, unsubstantiated bias, I realized through my mediations that she reminded me of one of my best friends' sister in high school who was incredibly mean-spirited, especially when it came to people's vulnerabilities.

I had a distorted, negative opinion about my body when I was a teenager. Many of my friends were bulimic and anorexic. Physically being of an average size, neither thin nor overweight, I felt fat in comparison to them. My friend's sister used to call me fat in the meanest possible way when she did not feel good about herself. I was the object on which she chose to release her self-loathing. Once I made the association that the German woman reminded me of my friend's anorexic sister, I could see how the mean-spirited girl's words were unconsciously seeded in my spirit, creating suffering for me. My experience with the German women opened my mind to questioning myself about where else in my life did I have bad feelings about people and things that I had not sorted out?

Once the lights went out in the evening, I checked in at work with my Blackberry. Under my blanket, I dimmed the screen light from my email. Every morning started the same way. I woke up early, made myself a cup of black tea, stretched, and then jogged for thirty minutes. I was one of two joggers on campus. Most people walked around the building in the morning. If I had extra time after running, I showered, dropped off my mat with my journal in the mediation room, and then went to breakfast. Once I finished eating breakfast, I climbed the staircase of a construction site to the top of a roof overlooking a long, winding river, where women handwashed the student's clothes. The wet tops and bottoms were placed on a rock to be hung later, surrounded by red clay ground that explained why some people's garments had a red hue.

Lunch consisted of beans, rice, naan bread, and vegetables with Indian sauces. There is something very liberating about participating in a silent retreat where there is no social obligation to greet or make small talk with someone. I walked to different areas of the compound to sit on tops of buildings to gaze at the river after lunch. One day, I reflected on how the river stood out as a symbol of my endless thoughts.

Mediating night and day, I could see how stubborn I could be. Even though I was divorced, regardless of my former husband's issues, I wanted to apologize to him for my piece in our discord. Graduation came too quickly. We celebrated jubilantly with music, dance, and laughter with the women Dasas.

At the end of the silent retreat, a group of us signed up to go to a hotel in Mamalapirum, a city with caves dating back to the 7th century. The luxury bus was filled with Germans, Italians, Americans, and Dutch, all Westerners. Our destination was recommended by friends who went through the program. Many of us chose to visit this old city because of a friend's pleasant experiences there.

The beachfront hotel we stayed in was beautiful. My friend from California stayed at the same hotel. We met in the evenings with the German woman for dinner. One night at my birthday dinner, I shared with the German women my bias and epiphany about how her presence during the silent retreat affected me. It was liberating to be able to share my transformation with her.

Our hotel was right on the beach. Running in the morning on the sand was difficult. Every day that went by, I ran less and less. There was a small Indian community living on the beach. Their boats sat still in formation, slowly swaying after one person would enter the water. I sat there, feeling such peace and contentment. Thankful for the life that I am blessed to lead, free of my daily professional ambition, engaging with other Westerners on a similar spiritual quest, centered me. Life was good.

Later that day, I hired a taxi to drive me to a temple. Once we were on our way, he stopped at a building, left the car running, and said, "I will be right back." I was curious as to why he needed to stop, and his absence felt long in the heat with the windows rolled down. He ran back into the driver's seat after ten minutes with a smile, thanking me for my patience. "Why did you need to stop?" I asked.

"I went to the Ganesh Temple to pray that we may be safe when traveling, praying that all obstacles be removed from our path." I liked this man and decided to hire him for one week to drive me to some of the most famous temples in Southern India.

First stop was the Shiva Srikalahasti Temple built in the 16th century, situated in Chittoor Southern India. It is an impressive building standing one hundred and twenty feet high, juxtaposed in a town with modern apartment buildings. Monkeys roamed freely around the grounds. I joined a group of people inside the temple, chanting for an undisclosed amount of time, stopping after my spirit felt elevated, inebriated in bliss. It occurred to me that I could sit there for hours, chanting, peacefully losing myself in the present with no Western agenda of moving on to my next place to maximize my day. This was enough. I felt satisfied.

One of my roommates from the Oneness University, a yoga teacher with long thick brown curly hair, was distressed when she found herself outside the temple with a panicking monkey entangled in her hair, trying to break free of her. She was equally upset until the small creature freed himself from her.

At the Arulmigu Ranganathaswamy temple lives a gentle female elephant, Andall. She is trained to kneel and raise her trunk as a friendly gesture. I stood in front of her watching, her gentle, engaging personality softening me when her trunk reached out to me. I closed my hand around a coin, extending it towards her. Her trick was to lift the currency from my hand with her trunk and lay it on the ground in front of us.

Families sat peacefully, looking at the Eastern and Western tourists on the vast grounds that house forty-nine Vishnu Temples, one of the Hindus' three revered deities. Vishnu is the preserver; Brahma is the

Creator; Shiva is the Destroyer. All three gods play an essential role in the Universe.

It felt peaceful strolling the compound, watching multigenerational families spending time together in a public, holy place. I appreciated the simplicity of their customs, quietly observing their surroundings with detachment.

A few days later, I traveled to Pondicherry to visit Sri Aurobindo Ashram. I toured the grounds and purchased books. Along the seaside, the streets were marked in French, remnants of a time in history when the French colonized the area.

With the little time we had left, we went to Auroville to see the famous golden sphere on the Ashram living grounds. We observed their accommodations, gardening, and retreat programs.

The abundance of historical architectural sites is impressive, so much so that it was easy to lose track of all the temples' names. More significant is how spirituality is steeped in all levels of life. Praying daily and trusting a higher power allows one to feel protected and loved by an unseen, omnipresent force. Many temples like the Badami Cave Temples and Karnataka carved from rocks were equally breathtaking in their magnificence.

India was a spiritually impactful experience. Three weeks of silence followed by a week of temple traveling and chanting reinforced the awareness that ninety percent of my suffering is self-inflicted through a chain of thoughts, with no awareness of the root cause for the feelings it conjures. I simply feel bad when I think of these repetitive thoughts. As I learn to observe my thoughts, the suffering I inflict upon myself by holding on to these beliefs can be released with more self-awareness. My outer world, people, things, and places reflect my inner world. What I believe I can experience or have is gated only by my thoughts. When my internal world changes, my outer world automatically starts changing. What I believe about life and myself is how my life will appear.

One of the most important lessons I learned is what happens to me emotionally when conflict arises. I used to believe that if a person said hurtful things to me, it was that person who made me feel bad. Then I learned it's not what the person said to me; it's my perception of what was said. If I try to fix someone else because of what he or she said, it can be extremely frustrating. It's much easier to look at the root of my feelings and where they come from, and why those words make me feel bad.

When I practice this, I learn not to take people's reactions personally. People can emote without my interpretation of what they are saying. I used to have a boyfriend for a short period who put me down all the time. I had no idea I was so incompetent until we dated. As strong as I was, I knew over time he would chip at my self-esteem.

One day, I went to him and said, "Hey, you seem to feel that there are many things wrong with me. I like who I am. And it is okay if you have issues with me."

"Are you breaking up with me?" he asked.

"I think we should stop seeing each other," I said. That was it. At first, I thought he was teasing me. Then the frequency of his comments didn't make me feel good about who I am. I had to ask myself, "Do you agree with his opinion of you?" I didn't. Arguing with him was pointless. It would only create more ill will, possibly escalating to saying mean things I couldn't take back. Once I realized I liked who I was, letting him go was easy. It made me happy.

My mind is a funny thing. Sometimes, when I jog around a field, I feel it symbolizes how my thoughts are an endless circle of bad feelings that don't make me feel good. Other times, I embrace the symbolism, the birth of my idea, the infinite loop, and the transformative root cause of a bad feeling.

taking a rickshaw to dinner

temple hoping in India

Kauai divorce family vacation before going to Maui

orchard in Makawao, Maui

watching the snorkeling nudist

snorkeling in Maui near the whales

Graduation from Academy of Intuitive Medicine

Geodesic Dome at Sri Aurobindo Ashram in Auroville

Arulmigu Ranganathaswamy Temple

the Cave Temples of Mahabalipuram

birthday celebration in Mahabalipuram India

FROM BAGHDAD TO BERKELEY

Conclusion

In 2016 after finishing up my business meetings in New York, I took the A train to uptown Manhattan after a full day of appointments. As I swayed back and forth on the train for a short time, the C train moved in a parallel direction. Tired, on a train with standing room only, I hung on to the metal bar in a mindless gaze watching the train accelerate past us. In every compartment stood a person who reminded me of myself at a different stage in my life in America. The little foreign girl, the rebellious teenager, the daughter, the businesswoman, the spiritual seeker, and the tourist. I am all of these people, these voiceless shadows staring back at me, reminding me how far I have come.

We are all a reflection of our community. This may be a prominent international city, countryside, clan, or tribe. Our cultural upbringing defines who we are. It allows us to have a bigger dream for ourselves or limits the scope of our opportunity.

My mother, teachers, and my Berkeley upbringing have enhanced my expectations and dreams for my life. I grew up in a place where my gender never defined who I was. I believed whatever I wanted to reach for was possible to grasp. For whatever reason, my mother thought it would be fine for me to travel through Europe by myself. She financed my biggest challenge, where I learned to make everyday decisions about where to go, what to eat, safety, and living conditions. I say this knowing it enrages some people. To me, she empowered me to see the world through an innocent lens, experiencing people's kindness and goodwill. The potential harm that came my way is no different than the harm that happens in our everyday communities.

I am an unconventional person in many ways. Yet my heritage does influence my conservatism. The voice that makes me pause and sometimes doubt myself because of what people may think comes from my Middle Eastern side. My Berkeley upbringing makes me believe that I can be anyone I want to be. My Irish heritage provides the perseverance and humor required to navigate uncertain times.

In my heart of hearts—I like who I am. My travels have privileged me with a lens that sees the world through a broader scope. The depth of my compassion and understanding for people runs as deep as the sea. Had I not had these opportunities to understand different lifestyles by immersing myself in their cultures, my view on the world would be much narrower.

My wish for you is to remember that tolerance unites us. I hope you open your mind to seeing and accepting people as they are, understanding that no matter how different they may appear, in the end, we all want the same thing, to feel safe, loved, and accepted by friends, family, and society.

this is where the journey begins with a courageous mother- Carol Louise Mc Feeley

birthday party at Aunt Grace's home in Bagdad in 1963- I am wearing the irish kilt with red hair on the left- Mimi is to the left of me, Jamal is sitting in the corner on the right and, John is across from me

mom, Mimi and I at John's Graduation in San Luis Obispo

*recreating our 1969 photo from top left to right- David, Ken, John, Joe
holding mom's ashes, Aunt Mary Grace, Jamal, Mimi, myself, Liz, Barbara,
Carolyn/Dusty and Paul*

Tribesman Grandfather Haji Jassim Al-Samarrie

Grandfather John Harold Mc Feeley – decedent of a clan from Donegal Ireland

last time I see dad in Baghdad in 2003

John, Mimi, Jamal and I at mom's memorial

we lost our sweet brother to diabetes complications when he was 53 years young

Mimi, John and I in Ireland

wearing Bibi's winter abya

California living

About the Author

Nadia Al-Samarrie is the author of *Sugar Happy: For Happy Blood Sugar Levels. Diabetes Health Guide* is her first semi-autobiographical medical diabetes book. She is a patient advocate, an AskNadia columnist, and publisher of the renowned DiabetesHealth.Com website.

From Baghdad to Berkeley: A Woman's Affair is her first auto-biography about her life as a bicultural Iraqi/Irish woman navigating her way through opposing cultures, racism, sexism, and independence.

nadiaalsamarrie.com

Twitter.com/Nadia Al-Samarrie@nsamarrie

Instagram.com/nadiaalsamarrie

DiabetesHealth.Com/AskNadia

Printed in Great Britain
by Amazon